One of the book's major strengths is its evidence-led exploration, blending theory with empirical analysis to considerable advantage. I can easily envisage using it for my MA teaching. This is a richly insightful treatment of pressing issues for visual journalism.

– Stuart Allan, Cardiff University

Visual Journalism and Verification at War

Considering the visual coverage of the war in Ukraine, this book provides critical insights into how newsrooms make use of visual materials, how visuals partake in journalistic storytelling in a modern wartime context, and how visual journalism practices affect the news media's role as arbiter of accuracy and ethics.

Based on a mixed-methods study, including analyses of selected visually driven news stories and interviews with media professionals in Norwegian and Swedish national media outlets, this book examines the news media's approach to the visual coverage of the war in Ukraine following the Russian invasion in 2022. The work is theoretically underpinned by ongoing boundary work within journalism and editorial negotiations over issues such as verification, source criticism, and trust; witnessing and ways of seeing; and ethical gatekeeping in photojournalism. At a juncture of rising concerns over AI, public distrust, and propaganda, this study adds a real-time aspect to these debates and reveals challenges as well as emerging strategies in the unfolding coverage. Furthermore, the comparative Scandinavian context serves to highlight points of tension between the global and the local and between those newsrooms relying on global image brokers and those conducting their own in-house reporting.

Written for researchers and advanced students of Visual Journalism and Conflict Reporting, this book is a timely intervention.

Maria Nilsson is Associate Professor of Journalism in the Department of Media Studies at Stockholm University, Sweden. Her research interests include visual storytelling, newsroom routines, the ethics of witnessing, visual representations of crises, and the history of photography. Her current research focuses on visual verification practices and disinformation and the truth claims of journalism in crisis coverage.

Anne Hege Simonsen is Associate Professor and Head of Department of Journalism and Media Studies at Oslo Metropolitan University, Norway. Her research interests include visual journalism, global and international reporting, climate crisis and environment coverage, media and minorities, physical walls and boundaries, and non-fiction writing. She has written, edited, and contributed to several text books in journalism for the Norwegian market.

Disruptions: Studies in Digital Journalism

Series editor: Bob Franklin

Disruptions refers to the radical changes provoked by the affordances of digital technologies that occur at a pace and on a scale that disrupts settled understandings and traditional ways of creating value, interacting and communicating both socially and professionally. The consequences for digital journalism involve far reaching changes to business models, professional practices, roles, ethics, products and even challenges to the accepted definitions and understandings of journalism. For Digital Journalism Studies, the field of academic inquiry which explores and examines digital journalism, disruption results in paradigmatic and tectonic shifts in scholarly concerns. It prompts reconsideration of research methods, theoretical analyses and responses (oppositional and consensual) to such changes, which have been described as being akin to 'a moment of mind-blowing uncertainty'.

Routledge's book series, *Disruptions: Studies in Digital Journalism*, seeks to capture, examine and analyse these moments of exciting and explosive professional and scholarly innovation which characterize developments in the day-to-day practice of journalism in an age of digital media, and which are articulated in the newly emerging academic discipline of Digital Journalism Studies.

The Institutional Development of Podcasting
From Participatory Projects to Platform Content
Aske Kammer and Thomas Spejlborg Sejersen

Visual Journalism and Verification at War
Norwegian and Swedish News Outlets Covering Ukraine
Maria Nilsson and Anne Hege Simonsen

For more information about this series, please visit: www.routledge.com/Disruptions/book-series/DISRUPTDIGJOUR

Visual Journalism and Verification at War

Norwegian and Swedish News Outlets Covering Ukraine

Maria Nilsson and Anne Hege Simonsen

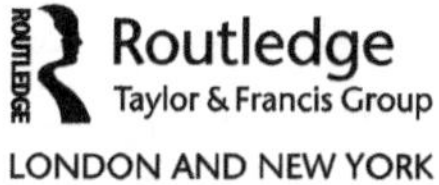

LONDON AND NEW YORK

First published 2025
by Routledge
4 Park Square, Milton Park, Abingdon, Oxon OX14 4RN

and by Routledge
605 Third Avenue, New York, NY 10158

Routledge is an imprint of the Taylor & Francis Group, an informa business

British Library Cataloguing-in-Publication Data
A catalogue record for this book is available from the British Library

Library of Congress Cataloging-in-Publication Data
Names: Nilsson, Maria Elizabeth, author. | Simonsen, Anne Hege, author.
Title: Visual journalism and verification at war: Norwegian and Swedish news outlets covering Ukraine / Maria Nilsson and Anne Hege Simonsen.
Description: London ; New York : Routledge, 2025. |
Series: Disruptions: studies in digital journalism |
Includes bibliographical references and index.
Identifiers: LCCN 2024058793 (print) | LCCN 2024058794 (ebook) |
ISBN 9781032763354 (hardback) | ISBN 9781032763347 (paperback) |
ISBN 9781003478072 (ebook)
Subjects: LCSH: Russian Invasion of Ukraine, 2022—Press coverage—Norway. | Russian Invasion of Ukraine, 2022—Press coverage—Sweden. | Russian Invasion of Ukraine, 2022—Mass media and the war. | Russo-Ukrainian War, 2014—Mass media and the war. | Photojournalism.
Classification: LCC DK5467 .N55 2025 (print) | LCC DK5467 (ebook) |
DDC 947.7086—dc23/eng/20241209
LC record available at https://lccn.loc.gov/2024058793
LC ebook record available at https://lccn.loc.gov/2024058794

ISBN: 9781032763354 (hbk)
ISBN: 9781032763347 (pbk)
ISBN: 9781003478072 (ebk)

DOI: 10.4324/9781003478072

Typeset in Times New Roman
by codeMantra

Contents

Figures

Tables

Acknowledgments

We wish to thank series editor Bob Franklin who encouraged and supported the idea at its early stage and helped guide us through the proposal phase, and Hannah McKeating at Routledge who made the production process smoother for us. The incisive comments from the reviewers of our proposal and manuscript were a tremendous help in making the project stronger and relevant. Thank you.

Along the way, we have benefitted from the feedback and encouragement from several colleagues and scholars. We are especially grateful to the members of the NordMedia Visual Communication and Culture temporary working group, a supportive and creative group of visual-studies scholars who nudged us forward when the project was at an impasse. Comments and discussion at panels at the Helsinki Photomedia Conference in 2024 were also decisive for our progress at a later stage.

Maria Nilsson would like to acknowledge the generous support from the Ann-Marie and Gustaf Anders Foundation for Media Research, which provided the valuable time to complete her part of the study. Each of us would also like to thank our respective home institutions, Oslo Metropolitan University (Anne Hege Simonsen) and Stockholm University (Maria Nilsson), for their support.

To the editors and photojournalists who took time from your busy schedule to talk to us and share your experiences: thank you for your invaluable contribution. Your reflections are the heart of this project.

And, finally, a heartfelt thank you to our families, John, Agnes, and Bjørn, for your patience and support, and to our dogs, Cajsa, Diva, Rossini, and Obi, for keeping us connected to the physical, tangible world.

Stockholm and Oslo in November 2024
Maria Nilsson and Anne Hege Simonsen

1 Disrupting the boundaries of photojournalism at war

War is disruptive. It is a social, economic, and political upheaval with destructive consequences for civilian populations and seldom contained within geographical borders. Most Europeans believed that territorial war belonged to the past in Europe when Russia invaded Ukraine in February 2022. The event was not only shocking in its own right. Small countries like Norway and Sweden were confronted with their own military and geopolitical vulnerabilities. Cultural, academic, and political cooperations with Russia were frozen or broken, economic sanctions were adopted, and military funds redirected to benefit the Ukrainian military struggle. In the news media, Russian president Vladimir Putin was framed as a possibly mad, power-hungry, and irrational leader, while Ukrainian president Volodymyr Zelenskyy was welcomed as a hero. In a spontaneous act of solidarity, several media outlets changed the names of Ukrainian cities from Russian-inspired to Ukrainian spelling (Kiev to Kyiv, Odessa to Odesa, etc.) and some journalists even inserted the Ukrainian flag as an act of solidarity. Refugees were welcomed in great numbers and with remarkably little debate, compared to, for instance, the Syrian refugees arriving in 2015. Ukrainians were allowed to bring domestic pets across the borders, cultural and educational differences were minimized, and Ukrainians were considered easy to integrate into the national workforce and in society at large. As one of our informants put it: "Ukraine is our backyard. Our audience identifies with the Ukrainians to an extent that I have never experienced [in war reporting] before".

The Russian full-scale invasion of Ukraine on 24 February 2022 is the first territorial war in Europe in 30 years with wide repercussions beyond the region, and it has been covered as such. Domestic concerns represent a huge part of the coverage in both countries yet there are some significant differences between Norway and Sweden. Russia is considered a national-security threat in both countries, but they lean on different strategies adopted at the end of World War II. Norway is a founding member of NATO and shares a border with Russia, while Sweden opted for continued neutrality. The war in Ukraine, however, prompted Sweden to apply for membership in the alliance, becoming a member in 2024. In editorial approaches towards the war theater

DOI: 10.4324/9781003478072-1

in Ukraine, however, the similarities are more poignant than the differences. The news media in both countries have chosen a strong on-location presence in Ukraine and, on occasion, news outlets from the two countries cooperate and reprint each other's material. The focus on presence differs from what has been common practice in their international conflict coverage for the last few decades, where most have relied primarily on international agencies (Gynnild 2017). Presence in the field further seems to be prompted not only by the war's political importance but also by professional disruptions within the journalistic field. With some minor exceptions, we therefore claim that it is possible to talk about a common perspective in their approach to the war in Ukraine.

Research into newsroom processes has shown that crises may instigate new challenges as well as new strategies (e.g. Olsson 2010; Usher 2009), in our case related to the complexities of the digital news environment and the influx of fake images. Visual materials play an exceedingly important role in journalistic war coverage, and the use of visual messages and social media by both sides of the conflict presents new opportunities and challenges for the news media. The early phase of the war was nick-named "The TikTok war" for the Ukrainian citizens' widespread use of social media to record videos and share their own experience of the Russian attack. Yet misinformation, unverified visuals, visual propaganda, and manipulated imagery also went viral, creating a challenge for journalists and the public to parse what was true and what was false (Mortensen & Pantti 2023, pp. 1–2).

This book examines how visual meaning, truth, and trust are negotiated in the visual coverage of the ongoing war in Ukraine. The aim is to examine how Norwegian and Swedish news media make use of visual materials produced by various sources, how visuals are positioned in journalistic storytelling in this modern war context, and how these circumstances affect the role of the news media as arbiters of accuracy and ethics.

We present original research conducted over the past two years, including 36 newsroom interviews and multimodal analyses of news coverage situated in the intersection between visual gatekeeping and the value afforded various visual sources and their news value. We examine photojournalism at war in multiple contexts: visual flows and visual meaning, gatekeeping in a context of blurred professional categories, and verification/source criticism of visual materials at a juncture of rising concerns with AI, distrust, and propaganda. This book contributes a regional focus that complements the Anglo-American dominance in journalism studies (Williams 2006). It studies and theorizes nodes of tension between relying on global image brokers and conducting in-house reporting. Another aim is to add to the growing scholarly interest in how visual journalism impacts the journalistic field (e.g. Caple 2019; Newton 2001). Furthermore, our book contributes a sustained focus on photojournalism and visually driven reporting from this conflict that we believe is missing in the international literature on the Russia-Ukraine war.

We use two key concepts in our study: visual meaning-making and witnessing, which bring out interesting aspects of boundary work and trust. Disciplinary boundaries are never constant and always subject to negotiation (Carlson 2019), and in our study we find them to have become exceedingly blurred. As a professional category, photojournalism has changed in dramatic and sometimes contradictory ways over the last few decades, having experienced cutbacks and marginalizations in newsrooms and also an increased interest in visual storytelling.

Trust is a key value in journalism and considered by many to be its most important capital. As the war in Ukraine is not fought only on the ground but is also considered an information war fought on social media and in legacy media alike, the growing focus on fact-checking and source verification has been the dominant way to secure the audiences' faith in the news media (e.g. Steensen et al. 2022; Waisbord 2018). In the current historical context, marked by rising concerns with AI, fake news, and distrust, in-house coverage seems to be an additional strategy to safeguard the fragile relation of trust between a media outlet and its audience, as in-house coverage represents more "old-fashioned" qualities, such as presence on the ground and editorial eyewitnessing.

In our empirical materials, we identified boundary negotiations and discourses about truth in different ways: in the global and local visual image streams intersecting in the coverage, blurring conceptions of the photograph and indexicality in the digital news; in the shifting roles of editors and photojournalists as witnesses and gatekeepers; and in visual verification routines where journalists seek to establish truth and trust in a climate of distrust.

A background to the full-scale invasion

The full-scale Russian invasion of Ukraine on 24 February 2022 was an escalation of a war that had been fought in eastern Ukraine since 2014, between Moscow-loyal separatist groups and Ukrainian forces, resulting in over 14,000 conflict-related deaths prior to the full-scale invasion, according to the United Nations.[1] The conflict ignited after the Euromaidan uprising and toppling of the Russian-friendly Ukrainian president Viktor Yanukovych in early 2014, followed by Russia's illegal annexation of Crimea the same year.

While prior to 2022, the conflict was a proxy war for Russia; on 24 February 2022, Russian forces entered Ukraine, according to Putin, to conduct a "special military operation" to "liberate" Ukraine from its "Nazi leadership".[2] (However, Ukrainian president Volodymyr Zelenskyy, who was elected in 2019, is Jewish). While the historical relationship between Ukraine and Russia is outside the scope of this book, post-Cold War geopolitical shifts have been described as the catalysts for the ongoing conflict, among those the Ukrainian approach to the west following its declaration of independence from the Soviet Union in 1991 and Russia's expansionist aspirations under Vladimir Putin, expressed in part in a resistance to Ukraine's aspirations to join the European Union and the NATO alliance (Balan 2022).

In the following section, we discuss literature and theoretical perspectives informing our study, including relevant research about the war in Ukraine; war photography; citizen witnessing and social media; visual verification and trust; photojournalism as witnessing; and the position of photojournalism and photography within journalism.

Previous research on the war in Ukraine

The geopolitics of the conflict and the centrality of communication strategies and propaganda have been in focus in scholarship on the conflict since 2014. Our study is informed, in particular, by European media and journalism scholarship about the current conflict.

Several studies focus on framing, including a study identifying frames in international coverage aligned with ideological perspectives and geopolitics, primarily critical of Russia before 2022 (Barthel & Burkner 2019), and patriotic framing found in the Ukrainian, Polish, Finnish, and Swedish reporting, also prior to 2022 (Nygren et al. 2018). An analysis of visually driven frames in television news (Ojala & Pantti 2017) found that, in the coverage of the Russian annexation of Crimea in 2014, news outlets in four European countries reproduced political frames in line with the respective countries' pro-Nato views. Research conducted after the full-scale invasion includes a study finding that the Swedish news media shifted, in 2022, to a position of consensus about Ukraine as a symbol of freedom, creating a blind spot for journalists (Nygren & Widholm 2024). Scholars taking a global perspective on the full-scale invasion (Bergman & Hearns-Branaman 2024, p. 4) argue that Western news media, especially in the U.S., have suppressed criticism of Ukraine.

Disinformation, propaganda, and the role of social media in the coverage and information flows is another area in the international research conducted prior to and after the Russian invasion in 2022. Contributions to a recently published anthology (Mortensen & Pantti 2023) include those focusing on how communication systems and infrastructure shape war coverage as a "hybrid information war". Another recent study found blurred boundaries between mainstream media, social media, and alternative media in information flows reaching the public (Nygren & Widholm 2024). Source criticism, though not primarily visual content (Nygren & Widholm 2022), was examined in another study finding that Swedish journalists relied on the fact-checking of international agencies and used disclaimers when publishing unverified social media content. Among the few available studies of the visual aspects of journalism in this conflict are one of the aforementioned titles (Ojala & Pantti 2017) and a study conducted by one of the authors of this book, focusing on

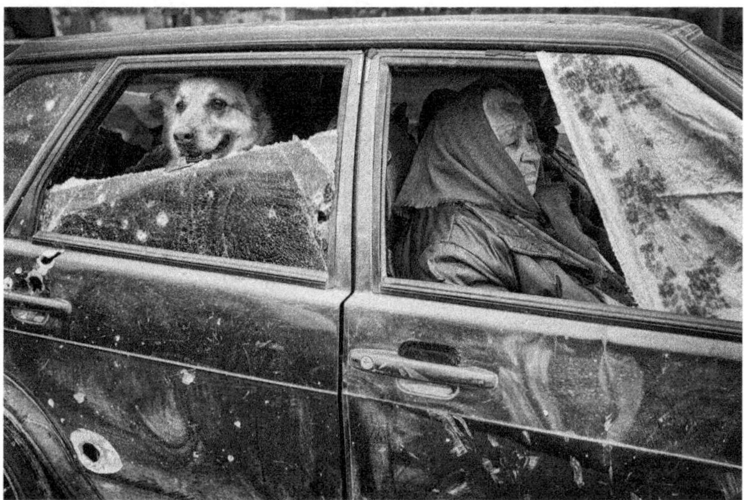

Figure 1.1 Evacuation of the town of Ruska Lozova north of Kharkiv on 29 April 2022. Hundreds of civilians came out of this war-crushed city, many after living in underground shelters for weeks. Photo by Eddy van Wessel. Reproduced with permission.

visual framing and gatekeeping during the first two months of the Russian invasion (Nilsson 2022).

Photojournalism at war, witnessing, and visual meaning-making

The professional prerogative of journalism to report from distant locations has historically relied on photography, with war coverage particularly reliant on the photographic eyewitness record (Allan 2014; Zelizer 2007). The photojournalist has to be on location and is closest to the events, and the photograph, through its realistic mode and emotional appeal, is a powerful conduit for empathy. According to Griffin: "As highly charged traces of conflict and mortal threat, images of war especially appeal to these human predilections for emotional identification" (Griffin 2010, p. 35). Images tend to reach the distant public first, contributing to shaping awareness and perspectives of events. Thus, war photographs carry the burden and expectation to show, reveal, and document war and its consequences. However, conflict photography is shaped by political structures as well as organizational routines and selection processes, in addition to circumstances on the ground in the theater of war. The photographic encounter is the result of selection and framing and is shaped by the news event, access, the assignment, the photographer's professional skills, and the personal encounter, belying a popular perception of the photographic moment and the image as transparent.

The gap between what photographs do and how they are perceived has fascinated scholars for generations. Barthes noted that we don't see photographs, only their content (Barthes 2000, p. 6), Sontag remarked that photographs have the status of found objects, as "unpremeditated slices of the world" that "are clouds of fantasy and pellets of information" (Sontag 1978, p. 69), while Blakely and Lloyd observed, as recently as 2021, that, according to colloquial understanding, photographs are still something that we *take* rather than *make* (Blakely & Lloyd 2021, p. 8). This balancing act between reality and art(ificiality) is also central to understanding the role of photojournalism within journalism.

The literature on war photographs in the news has focused in particular on visual framing (e.g. Brothers 1997; Fahmy & Kim 2008; Fahmy et al. 2014; Griffin & Lee 1995; Parry 2010). Media frames, understood as recurring patterns, have been attributed to factors ranging from ideology and geopolitics to editorial routines, for example, during the second Gulf War (Griffin 2010) when photographers and reporters were embedded with the allied troops, a factor impacting story topics, perspective, and access. Among the findings in the literature on Western conflict journalism are patterns aligned with national interests, so-called "patriotic journalism" (e.g. Greenwood & Jenkins 2015), and a lack of empathetic visibility for civilian victims in conflicts in the global south (e.g. Fürsich, 2010). The result, according to this literature, is a one-sided view of the conflict eliding the human cost and, potentially, the responsibility of the war-faring party or parties (e.g. Fahmy et al. 2014).

Witnessing and morality

Scholarly discussions about witnessing in Western media often entail ideas about morality and ethics that reflect *othering processes* in the media, both on the part of journalists/photojournalists in the field, editorial priorities, and media audiences (e.g. Allan & Peters 2014; Chouliaraki 2007; Eide & Simonsen 2007). This connection is explained by Chouliaraki as "the moralizing power of a particular way of seeing, witnessing, that organizes Western war and conflict reporting around demands for pity about human suffering rather than demands for justice over the causes of war" (Chouliaraki 2009, p. 215). Chouliaraki identifies witnessing functions as "the key mode of seeing" in Western media, thus responsible for reproducing human hierarchies that prioritize Western over non-Western suffering (Chouliaraki 2009, p. 215). This "hierarchy of victims" is relevant for the coverage of the war in Ukraine where *identification* seems to be a noteworthy entry point. Although not specifically mentioned by Chouliaraki, identification is a recognized news value (e.g. Galtung & Ruge 1965) and often understood as favoring cultural likeness or geographical proximity. Ukraine is not a Western country, but by way of the Russian invasion, the Ukrainians became Europeans. Our material suggests that, in contrast to e.g. Palestinians (present) and Syrians (2015), Ukrainians were understood more like *us* than *them,* despite the obvious cultural, political, and historical differences between Ukraine and Scandinavia, at least in the first phase of the war. Contrary to Chouliaraki and Stolic's (2017) findings related to visual renderings of Middle Eastern migrants and refugees in front-page images in 2015, where they concluded that the media visualizations "ultimately fail to humanize migrants and refugees" (p. 1162), Ukrainian refugees seem to have a maintained agency, as active participants in the war, even when fleeing (see Chapter 2 for further discussion).

While the critical literature on visual framing of conflict and the literature on witnessing appear to take different positions on the potential of the news photograph as a tool for visibility and agency, they also appear to share a normative expectation that it should be just that. This shared ambivalence towards the photograph has been articulated by Linfield: "Seeing does not necessarily translate into believing, caring, or acting. That is the dialectic, and the failure, at the heart of the photograph of suffering" (Linfield 2010, p. 33).

Similarly, Hariman and Lucaites (2016) note that photography is often criticized for not showing enough but also for showing too much. Considering photography as a public art, they write:

> Images are "partial, obscured, fissured and questionable," while viewers are constrained by many factors. Sometimes the best to hope for is that one can "steady ones' gaze," look at what is revealed, and speak on behalf of what is shown.
>
> (2016, p. 174, citing Boltanski)

Their point is, also drawing on the work of Azoulay (2012), that there is no pure photograph and no pure spectator. Proposing that photography is an anthropology of violence, Hariman and Lucaites consider it, "an important medium for understanding and confronting violence, in particular the violence of war" (p. 174). They nevertheless urge "humility" towards what is shown, and, like other scholars addressing witnessing, they place a responsibility on the viewer to assume a civic response (Azoulay 2012; Chouliaraki & Stolic 2017; Linfield 2010; Sliwinski 2011).

Frosh (2011), however, in a discussion of televised witnessing, describes the media as a tool of connectivity by which unknown others may be included in a cultural communion in a less invasive and threatening way than in real life. Frosh introduces the term "phatic morality", where suffering is one of many ingredients in a media consumer's daily news digest. "Phatic morality" maintains a certain distance and is less ambitious when it comes to providing a full engagement with the vulnerable other, but at least audiences are made aware of the predicaments of others within a framework of common humanity. Frosh is thus more concerned about the victims of war and inhuman conditions who are not present in the media at all, the "abjects". Being visible equals, from this perspective, being human.

Visual gatekeeping at war

The question of how the news media handle explicit conflict photographs is another area of focus in the literature on war photography, related to politics, morality, and ethics. As noted above, photographs showing the impact of conflict or crisis are often controversial because they suggest responsibility and are therefore frequently debated (Allan 2014; Morse 2014; Zelizer 2007). The literature on visual gatekeeping, the editorial processes for image production and selection, is not conclusive in its findings in this respect. Western news media have been found to be quite restrained (Ghersetti & Johansson 2021; Griffin & Lee 1995; Moriarty & Shaw 1995; Zelizer, 2010). However, research has also found that victims at a geographical distance might be shown less respectfully than those close to home (Hanusch 2012). Furthermore, there are cultural variations and differences, potentially or actually impacting selection as well as taboos and conventions, such as against showing images of "our" dead soldiers (e.g. Zelizer 2010). While intrusive visualizations, such as the famous photograph of the drowned Syrian boy Alan Kurdi widely circulated in 2015, have been criticized from an ethical standpoint (e.g. Mortensen et al. 2017), editorial strategies to withhold certain images have also been criticized as a form of self-censorship (Allan 2014).

Citizen witnessing

The digital shift and emergence of new technology for visual capture and sharing on social media in the past two decades have challenged the privileged position of journalism as the eyewitness to the public, while also providing new visual sources for crisis coverage (Patrick & Allan 2013; Zelizer 2007). Labels such as *connective witnessing* (Mortensen 2016) highlight the media's ability to create "multiple connections between individuals, groups, and societies in a mediatized networked environment" (Hoskins 2011, in Kot et al. 2024). This has made the relationship between the individual and the collective aspects of witnessing more dynamic and fluid. It has also caused scholars to question the view of journalists as the main gatekeepers of information reaching the public (Schwalbe et al. 2015).

Today, journalistic gatekeeping boundaries are negotiated and challenged in the digital culture where many gatekeepers reach publics independently of journalism (Mortensen, 2016). According to some scholars, editors today are more akin to curators or gate-checkers, as the news media produce less content in-house (Caple 2019; Gynnild 2017; Schwalbe et al. 2015). While news outlets source social media for stories and use the content in their coverage, verification has been identified as a gatekeeping strategy among news outlets today (Bjerknes 2022). Global news agencies, the dominant players in international coverage, have been found to adapt to a social-media environment where they are no longer first in the "information chain" in part by developing expertise in verification as a way to assert credibility and truth (Jukes 2022)

The literature on so-called citizen eyewitnessing emerging in the past few decades has addressed practices ranging from activists in authoritarian contexts providing journalistic content and proof to "accidental photojournalists" (Allan 2014, p. 3) who happen to witness or experience a crisis or accident, capture it visually, and share on social media. Eyewitness visuals made by members of the public have been found to possess authenticity and proximity, in some cases found superior to professional imagery (Allan 2014; Andén- Papadopoulos & Pantti 2013; Patrick & Allan 2013). The various perspectives available to the public may challenge the formerly privileged eyewitnessing position of journalism through photography while also offering content with different perspectives (Frosh & Pinchevski 2014; Zelizer 2007). This can also be seen as an increased transparency where competing viewpoints are available to the public (Caple & Bednarek 2016; Harcup & O'Neill 2017).

While research addressing the emergence of citizen witnessing about two decades ago emphasized its democratizing potential, a current concern is a rising culture of distrust and propaganda (Chouliaraki & Al-Ghazzi 2022). The prediction in the literature, that photojournalists would be made obsolete by citizen witnesses, is not borne out in a conclusive way (e.g. Nilsson & Wadbring 2015). Research into war coverage has found that journalists assert their gatekeeping power for stated ethical or verification purposes when it comes to images (Andén-Papadopoulos & Pantti 2013; Nilsson 2019; Patrick & Allan 2013). Images made by an eyewitness may be seen as too intrusive, too close, to make the cut for publication in a newspaper (Morse 2014). Thus, journalists remain "central players" (Vos 2020) as gatekeepers in the production of news with considerable power in that process.

Visual verification, trust, and truth

Journalistic witnessing contributes to a collective understanding of conflict, sometimes in accordance with and sometimes in opposition to other accounts, such as reports from affected civilians or academic analyses (Kot et al. 2024). However, journalism's claim on truthful reporting has been severely challenged with the influx of fake news, fake imagery, and falsifications where real events are presented within fictitious frameworks, sometimes mimicking journalistic presentation modes. As noted by Ireton and Posetti, the goal of disinformation is not necessarily to convince audiences that the false content is true "but to impact on agenda setting (on what people think is important) and to muddy the informational waters" (2018, p. 10).

In the digital media landscape, verification has become a favored tool in countering mis- and disinformation. It is also an important boundary value in journalism, and verification can be seen as a strategy to preserve what Carlson has labeled "journalistic authority" (Carlson 2017). Verification has triggered an increasing interest in visual truth claims in journalism, as a way to rebuff falsifications (e.g. Hahn & Stalph 2018; Khan et al. 2023; Thomson et al. 2022), in the use of news photographs as forensic tools for investigations of human rights violations and for news coverage about such alleged crimes. This is a practice with historical antecedents, for example, when photographs were used as evidence in the Nüremburg trials against Nazi leaders and more recently in investigations before the ICC (Sliwinski 2011).

Visual verification methods, often referred to as Open Source Intelligence (OSINT), examine metadata and forensic aspects of an image, such as location and time of day, in relation to verifiable data from other sources e.g. weather reports, face recognition tools, revised image search, etc. As such they concentrate on the image as a document and not so much on the meaning-making aspects of the content, which may still be misleading. Another dilemma, as pointed out by Steensen et al. (2022), is that the verification discourse is dominated by binary terms such as accurate or inaccurate, reliable or unreliable, "while not adequately acknowledging that degrees of accuracy and reliability depend on socio-cultural context and interpretation" (2022, p. 2123). Steensen et al. echo Waisbord's (2018) concern about how the media's role as a trustworthy source of information is declining, not exclusively because of outside manipulation but also related to epistemological structures embedded within journalism. In his view, the objectivist tradition in journalism relates to a positivist worldview, "disciplining knowledge by promoting the scientific model as the only legitimate knowledge" (2018, p. 1869), ideologically connected to the new world order after the World War II. However, notions of objectivity as a professional goal are increasingly being challenged in a networked and multivocal society, where "more horizontal dynamics and multiple flows of information in public communication foster skepticism, dissident, and critical views that do not conform to the premises of scientific knowledge or the foundational elements of journalistic epistemology" (ibid, p.1871). According to Waisbord, "truth makes sense in context, as part of discursive conditions that determine the correspondence between news and reality" (ibid, p. 1872). Another effect of the muddied informational waters is, as Capilla observes, that "truth is being replaced by sincerity, as an epistemological value, in people's understanding of the news" (Capilla 2021, p. 313), thus highlighting the role of public trust in an identifiable originator.

According to Carlson, however, journalistic objectivity should not be seen as naïve empiricism but as a "learned position" rooted in an understanding of professionalism, which he calls "practiced distance" (Carlson 2019, p. 1120). In our context, it should be further mentioned that Scandinavian journalism comes from a slightly different tradition than e.g. American and British news media. In Scandinavian journalism, *source criticism* as a method is taught in journalism schools and represents a core professional value (Steensen et al. 2022). Source criticism represents a somewhat softer approach to journalistic truth claims, based on the notion that all sources have a tendency and that interpretation is an important part of the journalistic toolkit.

Ambivalence towards photography in journalism

Even if the so-called *visual turn* (Mitchell 1994; Rose 2023; Sturken & Cartwright 2018) in journalism has made photography and other visuals essential to almost every kind of reporting (Caple 2019), the status of the visual already has a long history of ambivalence within the profession. Cherished for their ability to document, illustrate, and enliven a reportage or a news story, photographs have also been deemed voyeuristic, propagandistic, and emotionally loaded (Sontag 1978). Written text has traditionally trumped photography in the hierarchy of journalistic modalities. Traditionally, leading positions in media institutions have often been held by people with no visual background (e.g. Bjerknes 2012; Moses 2000), and newsroom cultures have to a large extent shared a view of photography as predominantly illustrative and secondary to text (e.g. Bjerknes 2012; Simonsen & Evensen 2017; Zelizer 2010). Yet, as photography required specialized technological and storytelling skills, photographers managed to carve a space as a separate discipline for in-house press photographers. In a Scandinavian setting, the concept of the photojournalist as an equal within the journalistic field is of more recent origin (Knudsen in Fonn, 2015, p. 153), as the traditional "press photographer" was mainly commissioned to photograph what the writing reporter deemed most important.

However, as pointed out by Carlson (2017), journalism is a profession particularly dependent upon its technological conditions and, as digitization affected the news industry deeply, photojournalists were arguably especially affected; new technology made capturing photographs and live footage technically easy, and economically challenged media outlets opted for cutbacks in their photo departments (Anden-Papadopoulos & Pantti 2013; Ferrucci et al. 2020; Gynnild et al. 2017; Mortensen & Keshelashvili 2013). Citizen-produced photographs and videos, multiskilled reporters who could simultaneously write and take pictures/footage, and even stock photo agencies were expected to replace photojournalists (Caple 2019; Nilsson & Wadbring 2015).

Scholarly ambivalence towards photojournalism

Photojournalism and imagery also have an ambiguous position within media scholarship. Media representations are multimodal by definition, yet they are often referred to as multimodal *texts* (Kress & Van Leeuwen 2006; Skovholt & Veum 2022), implicitly making words the preferred objects of analysis and other communication modalities wanting or supplementary. This view has been challenged among others by Mitchell (2005) who warns against analytical purity in media analysis. In his view, all media are mixed media, made up of different blends of materials and technologies, skills, habits, social spaces, institutions, and markets. Some elements may be dominant or subordinate, some media may be nested within another, and some braided or sutured onto another.

Within media and journalism studies, journalistic texts are by far the preferred object of study compared to journalistic images. This can partly be linked to their different communicative qualities. Written text is unilinear and semantically "rational", whereas images are multivocal and polysemic. Textual elements may seem easier to control analytically, even if textual meaning may be just as layered and contextually entangled as images.

Digital image flows and human interpreters

While the single photograph has been the preferred object of photo theory, the digital turn has led to a call for theoretical renewal (Henning 2018). In the media, images are increasingly talked about in terms like "flows" and "streams". As digitally born photographs appear in "series, repetitions, sequences, rapid volleys" (Lister in Rubinstein & Sluis, 2013, p. 154), Rubinstein and Sluis suggest that digital photography no longer produces meaning through indexicality or representation but rather through "the aggregation and topologies of data" (ibid, p. 156). They consider the effects of the mathematical encoding of visual content into metadata as particularly salient, as metadata leaves little space for "ambiguity, negation and otherness". Rubinstein and Sluis' fear is that images will be drained of their potential political agency, which, according to them, "depends on the possibility of a multitude of interpretations, ambiguities and differences" (ibid, 2013, p.154).

In a comprehensive article on visual media flows, Henning (2018) warns against a sharp theoretical breach between analog and digital approaches to photography. She maintains that there is room for both and stresses that theories of flow in relation to media "are theories of human cognitive processes as well as of technologies", since they "bring together questions of consciousness, attention and perception with technical structures that are built in, hardwired or designed into different media" (2018, p. 139). Henning further points to the ideological dimensions of the flow concept and how it links to notions of continuity and freedom of choice on the one hand, yet is perceived as linear, unstoppable, rapid, endless, and instant on the other. She reminds us, "Flow [...] is not smooth and seamless or soporific, it is jarring, jagged, disruptive, and exciting. This is all about the rhythm and pace of perception and interpretation and attention" (2018, p. 142).

While we agree on the potential for depleted meaning in image flows where machines perform both coding and decoding, we subscribe to the view of Henning, and we would oppose taking people and the social context out of the equation. Regarding the visual news flow from Ukraine, we find a multitude of human actors, as more or less professional photographers in the field and as curators and gatekeepers in the newsrooms, filtering the visual messages before they are transmitted to audiences. Social media is also basically a human source and an important channel for photographs and footage from non-professionals. In fact, satellite imagery may be the only visual source that can be classified as purely technological, but even satellite images are distributed and interpreted by humans.

Our empirical study

Our aim with this book is to contribute empirically to the literature on photojournalism, visual verification, and witnessing in a period of disruptions for the news media and to the literature on the war in Ukraine. A dual aim is to advance theory and method for visual research. In particular, we believe there is a need for developing methods for visual analyses of digital information and visual flows. Furthermore, we believe that the current disruptions to the role of journalism and conceptions of the image and visual truth need to be further theorized.

Specifically, in order to explore visual meaning-making processes and witnessing in the coverage of the war in Ukraine, we have designed and conducted a study of selected news outlets in Norway and Sweden. While the war in Ukraine dates back at least to 2014 and the Russian annexation of Crimea, our empirical focus starts with the Russian full-scale invasion in February 2022 and extends throughout 2024 for the interviews conducted, while the study of published material is focused on the first 12 months after the invasion, in particular the first two weeks as well as the massacre in Bucha discovered in April 2022.

Empirical focus

Norway and Sweden are part of the five-nation Nordic region that shares cultural and political histories and commonalities in media policy, known as the "Nordic model" (Syvertsen 2014, cited in Mathisen 2023, p. 7). Specifically, the welfare state developed in these countries in the 20th century placed journalism "between the state and the market" (Mathisen 2023, p. 7). In this model the state is an active and proactive agent that gives high priority to public-service media. The approach aims to "secure the enlightenment role of the media, and to support cultural production to survive in small markets with national languages" (Bruun & Münter Lassen 2024, p. 13). The idea of a Nordic exceptionalism has been questioned given that the region is affected by globalization, and, in the field of journalism, the dominant media organizations operate according to a corporate logic. There are nevertheless a number of characteristics of the news media's position and relationship to the public in the region. These include public-service media, media subsidies, the notion of journalism as "a public good" (Allern & Pollack 2017), and comparably high news consumption and trust in journalism (Røe Mathisen 2023). Another characteristic of the news outlets in this region is that the tabloids, compared to, for example, those in the U.K., are considered less sensationalistic in their methods and, for instance, in their use of explicit imagery.

While news outlets in Norway and Sweden are regional and rely primarily on agency content for international coverage (Gynnild et al. 2017; Nygren & Widholm 2022), public-service broadcast and some of the larger news outlets have international correspondents. Smaller outlets may assign reporters and photographers to cover international stories on a short-term basis. However, the largest news organizations in the two countries increased their in-house coverage and assigned teams to travel to Ukraine in the past two years. This increased international focus, from a visual point of view, was part of the inspiration for our study.

It was important for us to focus on news outlets that have a visual area/photo desk and that have had their own reporters and photographers on assignment in Ukraine since the invasion. Thus, we wanted to capture strategies for coverage and selection of agency material as well as the newsrooms' own material made by staff photographers or freelancers. Our selection criteria further included size and reach. As a result, we included broadcasts and the largest national-circulation newspapers in each country.

The selected news outlets in Norway are the largest circulation national media outlets *Verdens Gang (VG)*, *Aftenposten*, *Dagbladet*, and the two biggest broadcast services, the public-service NRK and the commercial public-service TV 2.[3] *VG* and *Dagbladet* will be referred to as tabloids, while *Aftenposten* is a former broadsheet with a subscription-based circulation. Defined by digital reach to a population of 5.5 million people, by the end of 2022, *VG* was the biggest news outlet in Norway, followed by NRK and *Dagbladet* in second and third place, TV 2 as number five, and *Aftenposten* as number nine. By circulation, *VG* is the biggest, followed by *Aftenposten* and *Dagbladet*. As shown in Table 1.1, Norwegian media has experienced some stagnation between 2022 and 2024, which is relevant to our study since it has led to cutbacks and reorganization of newsrooms (see also Chapter 3).

Table 1.1 Norwegian media by reach in 2022 and 2024[4]

No.	*News outlet*	*Daily reach 2022 Q4*	*Daily reach 2024 Q3*
1	*VG*	1,957,961	1,908,916
2	NRK	1,540,451	1,334,605
3	*Dagbladet*	1,359,733	1,105,022
5	TV 2	1,127,162	8,49,929
9	*Aftenposten*	377,050	3,53,466

Table 1.2 Swedish media by reach in 2022 and 2024

No.	*News outlet*	*Daily reach 2022 Q4*	*Daily reach 2024 Q2*[a]
1	*Aftonbladet*	3,751,000	3,665,000
2	*Expressen*	2,460,000	2,338,000
3	SVT.se	1,641,000	1,354,000
5	*Dagens Nyheter*	871,000	821,000
9	*Svenska Dagbladet*	655,000	593,000

Source: https://www.kantarsifo.se/sites/default/files/reports/documents/rackviddsrapport_orvesto_konsument_2024_2.pdf https://www.kantarsifo.se/sites/default/files/reports/documents/rackviddsrapport_orvesto_konsument_2022_2.pdf

[a] The most recent available figures for 2024 measure 1 May–31 August.

The selected Swedish outlets are the public-service television Sveriges Television (SVT), and the four largest-circulation national newspapers, *Dagens Nyheter (DN)* and *Svenska Dagbladet*, and the two leading tabloids, *Aftonbladet* and *Expressen*. Among the Swedish outlets, *DN* and *Svenska Dagbladet* will be referred to as subscription-based outlets, and *Aftonbladet* and *Expressen* as tabloids.

Aftonbladet had the largest digital reach of all Swedish news outlets in 2022, to a population of 10.5 million people. *Expressen* was in second place, public-broadcast *SVT* in third place,[5] *DN* fifth, and *Svenska Dagbladet* sixth. Measured by newspaper circulation, in 2024, *DN* was the largest, *Aftonbladet* second-largest, *Expressen* third, and *Svenska Dagbladet* fourth. Table 1.2 shows digital reach for Swedish news outlets 2022 and 2024 with a similar stagnation to that found among the Norwegian news outlets.

Methods

Methodologically, we address different relational and contextual aspects of journalistic visual storytelling in war, through interviews, visual, and bi-modal analyses and insights from conceptual debates. Specifically, in the first empirical chapter (Chapter 2), we draw on a conceptual discussion of multi-sourced image flows to address journalistic witnessing modes in published multi-image constellations. As mentioned above, "image flows" and "news streams" are considered a marker of today's media ecology. As a methodological contribution to these aspects of witnessing and visual meaning-making in journalism, we pursued visual and bi-modal analyses of selected published materials. In Chapter 3, we use the concept of gatekeeping to analyze professional roles and interview respondent perceptions of witnessing. In the final empirical chapter, Chapter 4, the conceptual input comes from writings on epistemology in journalism and notions of truth and trust.

Our combination of methods aims to triangulate and strengthen the findings and to compensate for the weaknesses of using a single method. This is primarily a qualitative study, aiming to address reflections and perceptions of respondents as well as how witnessing and visual meaning-making processes flow. We have conducted a quantitative overview as a supplement, laying the groundwork for the qualitative analyses aiming to familiarize us with the extensive visual materials published.

We prioritized the first two weeks of the full-scale invasion, beginning on 24 February and concluding on 9 March, and a second period, the week news broke about the massacre in Bucha. For Bucha, we chose to focus on 3–10 April, to cover the day when the story broke and the first week, which was heavily covered in the news.

Our rationale for choosing these two periods was to capture important breaking news events and periods when the news outlets were on location in Ukraine. Another important factor was that challenges of disinformation and verification as well as ethical questions about explicit pictures of casualties could be expected to emerge in these periods.

Visual and bi-modal analyses

Quantitatively, the war in Ukraine was covered in phases, with a massive interest starting with the rumors of a possible invasion in early February 2022, followed by the actual outbreak. The main peak was in week 9 of 2022 (28 February–6 March) with almost 60,000 news entries in total for all Norwegian and Swedish media.[6]

The coverage later "normalized" at a lower intensity level but with smaller peaks representing strategic and significant events at the frontline. According to Boyko and Horbyk (2023), the Ukrainian news media responded to the war in three phases: total mobilization (from 24 February 2022 until the de-occupation of Northern Ukraine in April), plateau (April to October 2022 where war became part of daily life), and blackout (from October 2022: infrastructural turmoil as a result of Russian strikes on critical infrastructure with digital communication tools becoming less reliable). These phases seem to correspond quite well with the Scandinavian coverage in our analysis. A final important observation is that the Israeli war in Gaza, starting with the Hamas attack on 7 October 2023, did not lead to the significant drop in news stories from Ukraine that could have been expected. Even if the war in Gaza dominated headlines and in-house stories in the Scandinavian news outlets and several outlets did not prioritize traveling to Ukraine for many months, the war in Ukraine maintained a significant media interest.

In all, our main quantitative corpus (24 February–9 March 2024) consists of 4,881 news stories registered in the Retriever media archive, which covers print and online editions for the newspapers and digital news sites for television. We used the broadly outlined search terms "Ukraine" in connection with "conflict" or "war", omitting stories reporting on domestic issues.

A substantial part of the broadcast coverage is thus not included in the research material. However, according to Bruun & Münter Lassen, broadcast online services function as an integral part of the broadcast companies' "herding" strategies, aimed to convince audiences to stay "within their own portfolio of channels and services while the use of broadcast television is dwindling" (2024, p. 4). The visual war coverage on these sites is thus not without interest.

The quantitative samples were analyzed to be able to say something about frequency and potential variations between our selected media outlets, image source (in-house, agency, social media, satellite, or other), genre (breaking news, reportage, or other), and whether published material was produced on the home desk or originated in the field. We also noted the number of still photo and live footage entries as well as content according to gender representation and main topic (leaders, civilians, military, physical destruction, or other). However, there is some variation in how the material is presented in the Retriever archive. As an example, all outlets produce short newsfeed entries, but for some media, these are not registered in Retriever. Some have the newsfeeds archived as a separate category, while some don't. Furthermore, some news outlets produce fewer and more edited stories, while others present a dynamic mix of short and long articles. This makes it difficult to present statistical comparisons regarding the scope of the coverage in a meaningful way. As this is primarily a qualitative study, we settled for an observational approach where we scrolled through all the material and focused on identifying the field reports produced by the news outlets' own teams. In this category we also included freelance material and special reports from Ukrainian civilians that were clearly commissioned by the home desk as well as stories produced as a collaboration between a team in the field and the home desk. For both weeks, this yielded a total of 81 stories in the paper editions and 162 in the online editions. The content overlaps to a high degree between these two categories, and we found more unique stories in the online editions. From a visual perspective, however, there are several interesting variations in how the same material is presented online and on paper (see Chapter 2).

We also looked specifically at the coverage of the massacres in Bucha and Borodyanka in April 2022 and at the stories published online at the one-year mark. For Bucha and Borodyanka, our main concern was qualitative aspects of visibility related to the news reports and also how visibility affects the numerical coverage (see Figure 2.2 in Chapter 2). Regarding the stories at the one-year mark, our aim was to explore the formation of visual tropes and symbolic aspects in the coverage. Here, we selected the most prominent commemorative story from each outlet and conducted a close reading of the material as well as a comparative analysis (see Chapter 2).

Interviews

Through semi-structured interviews, we aimed to capture perceptions of strategies, challenges, and goals in the coverage. The respondents were selected through purposeful/strategic selection, on the basis of their roles and experience covering Ukraine since the Russian invasion. We focused on leadership roles in terms of decisions about visual coverage as well as relevant positions in image production and selection. The main focus was on the visual area of the newsrooms, yet we also sought to include informants who work with and make publication decisions about the incoming image flows. We interviewed heads of visual areas, photo editors, foreign editors, news editors or equivalent, and photojournalists in the two countries. By interviewing photojournalists, we highlight the perspective of the professionals who are on location and who interact most closely with people affected by events, a dimension we believe is frequently overlooked in research into editorial processes. Equally important was to interview photojournalists about their perceptions of roles since their professional subgroups have been particularly affected by structural changes in the industry, leading to eliminations of positions and re-definitions of the role of professional photographers.

Since our selected news organizations differ in size and mission as well as routines and use of visuals, the function, and title of those interviewed varied between newsrooms. We interviewed a total of 28 editors and 8 photojournalists, including staff photographers and freelancers contributing to our selected outlets and other outlets. Our interviews were conducted face-to-face when possible, otherwise digitally. The conversations were guided by an interview guide created and used by both researchers to ensure that corresponding themes were covered. Respondents were assured ahead of time and at the start of the interviews that they would be anonymous to ensure they could speak freely. Anne Hege Simonsen conducted all the interviews in Norway, while Maria Nilsson conducted those in Sweden, and each of us transcribed their own interviews and translated them into English. All interviews, except one conducted in English, were conducted in Norwegian or Swedish, in the respective countries. The findings from the interviews were analyzed and presented in Chapters 3 and 4, topically organized according to the interview questions and the themes and topics emerging from the interviews. Specifically, the interview findings included in Chapter 3 address witnessing, explored through the lens of routines and professional roles and status. In Chapter 4, findings from our interviews with editors are used to discuss perceptions and strategies for verification and source criticism as well as respondents' views on disinformation.

The semi-structured interview is a suitable method for our study because it allows for a certain openness and flexibility in the conversation, enabling a deeper exploration, and the discovery of important topics the researcher may not have considered ahead of time. In terms of our topic, interviews also give insights into editorial processes, through the perceptions of respondents. To be clear, the semi-structured interview does not reveal actual processes, in our case newsroom processes. Rather, it gives us the respondents' perceptions and views about those processes. As professional interviews, they also inform us about professional knowledge, experience, and perception of roles. As a result, by interviewing a cohort of professionals, we gain a rich perspective of a professional culture. However, the method also has limitations. The interview situation is a constructed setting separated from the practice that is discussed. Furthermore, respondents may be reluctant to offer criticism. We sought to mitigate this by offering anonymity and by interviewing a substantial number of respondents—a total of 36 interviews in our case—and by including a roster of several individuals from each professional category. Furthermore, respondents sometimes independently concurred on certain topics, an indication that a response was not merely a subjective or personal opinion but rather a professionally informed response. During our analysis of the interview transcripts, we also found that certain answers repeated themselves, indicating that we had interviewed a sufficient number of respondents.

The interviews were carried out from late 2022 until mid-2024 because we aimed to capture processes and changes in real time as well as the phases of the war and the experience of journalists covering an ongoing crisis. One example of a change occurring during our research period were newsroom initiatives for visual verification that emerged as a response to the challenges of disinformation in this war. Another beneficial outcome of this approach has been that respondents interviewed more recently have a perspective that allows them to look back on and reflect critically on changes and challenges in the early coverage and other topics. The methodological implication of our strategy is that it's difficult to compare the newsrooms. However, this was not our intention.

Chapter outline

Chapter 2 addresses the editorial usage of agency and in-house material in three different contexts from the first year of the full-scale invasion, namely the outbreak of war, the massacres in Bucha/Borodyanka discovered in April the same year, and the one-year mark, in February 2023. The theoretical focus is on the performative aspects of visuals from different sources in multimodal journalistic storytelling as well as their narrational relations to the home audiences. In the chapter, we critically address notions of image flows and news streams and look at how images migrate across time and space, finding significant contrasts between the coverage from the visually (and politically) chaotic first week and the concentrated coverage of the atrocities in Bucha some weeks later. At the one-year mark, we found few iconic images and the tropes identified mostly evaded a stereotypical visualization of refugees and people affected by war.

In Chapter 3, we continue our examination of witnessing, through findings from our interviews with 28 editors and 8 photojournalists focusing on their experiences of the in-house coverage from Ukraine. The interviews contributed a real-time perspective of the coverage of an ongoing conflict, which we believe was of significant value for the study. Using gatekeeping (Shoemaker & Vos 2009) as our concept, the chapter looks at aspects of routines and witnessing and how they were affected in the coverage of this conflict. We identified three salient themes: being on location and keeping the public at home engaged, witnessing and showing the human cost of war, and handling access and bias.

Chapter 4 is theoretically grounded in literature on journalistic truth claims in the intersection between fact-checking, source criticism (Steensen et.al. 2022; Waisbord 2018), and classic photo-theoretical debates on visual truth claims (e.g. Naas 2011; Newton 2001; Sontag 1978). Based on findings in our interviews, we discuss how visuals form a part of the strategic response of the news outlets in relation to the decreasing authority of journalism (Carlson 2017). Our findings show that the news outlets have adopted several strategies to counter distrust in their visual coverage that may briefly be summarized as skilling up and establishing a hierarchy of trust. These include a collaborative verification in Norway servicing all news outlets, and smaller such initiatives in Sweden started by two individual outlets, a contrast in approaches between the two countries.

The fifth and concluding chapter discusses our empirical findings, specifically verification expertise and a hierarchy of trust; a negotiation between global and local boundaries in different narrative logics; and the role of journalists as witnesses and gatekeepers. Addressing the implications of our findings more broadly, we discuss the sharing of resources across media outlets as a perceived necessity emerging in global crises and journalistic presence on location as part of a contract with the public and a way to build and maintain a relationship of trust with readers.

Funding and approvals

The study has been reviewed and approved by the research ethics boards of Norway and Sweden.

The Swedish part of the study, conducted by Maria Nilsson, is supported by an external research grant from The Ann-Marie and Gustaf Anders Foundation of Media Research (Ann-Marie och Gustaf Anders stiftelse för medieforskning). The Norwegian part has not received external funding.

A note on our collaboration

All chapters in this book are co-written by Maria Nilsson and Anne Hege Simonsen as main authors, with an equal empirical, methodological, and theoretical input. We have been equal partners from the idea and proposal stages to the design and realization of the study, the analysis of the materials, and throughout the various phases of writing, editing, and revision.

Notes

1 https://war.huri.harvard.edu/background/
2 https://war.huri.harvard.edu/background/
3 https://info.tv2.no/info/artikkel/in-short
4 https://medietall.no/?liste=persontall&r=PERSONTALL&pid=53545&p=2409&gs=1&g_sels=
5 The reach for SVT here refers to the digital news site svt.se. Numbers for the reach of SVT as a whole are measured as reach of part of the population with SVT reaching 83% of the population in 2023, compared to 84% in 2022. Source: https://siffror.svt.se/det-har-vill-svt.html
6 These numbers are derived from the database and media archive Retriever. Our search words were "Ukraine" and the category was "war and conflict".

2 Bridges and flows

Journalism is commonly referred to as "history in the making", and the Russian invasion of Ukraine was understood by most parties as a particularly disruptive and transformative historic event. During the first couple of months, Ukraine was the main story in all news outlets in our study. As one informant in a Norwegian tabloid said: "The whole newsroom became a foreign news desk." The main visual themes were fight, flight, and civilian suffering.

The number of still images, live footage, maps, and other visuals from Ukraine is enormous. In addition to the coverage by Norwegian and Swedish teams, the newsrooms had access to images from international agencies, partisan news agencies, social media, private individuals, and satellite imagery. While the academic literature on the role of images in war reporting tends to focus on the single image (Chouliaraki 2017, p. 1163; Hariman & Lucaites 2007; Allan & Zelizer 2004, p. 115), we find from 0 to 15 images or visual elements in the news stories in our samples. The single image is rare. This calls for a scrutiny of concepts like image flows and news streams. As noted by Henning (see Chapter 1), there is a tendency to overstress the fluidity in these concepts as uninterrupted and disregard what she calls "the jarring, jagged and disruptive" dimensions of flows (Henning 2018, p. 142). Our take on this is to investigate image flows as networks and look at how different types of imagery from the Ukrainian war are produced and disseminated through them. In published contexts, the images constitute meaning-making elements in visual/textual configurations, in newspaper spreads or online. The variation in such configurations is huge, and it is beyond the scope of this study to map them, but we will point to some identifiable aspects related to production site and production time.

Images may be used as conceptual illustrations, documentation/proof, or spaces of reflection. Photojournalists, however, seldom control the publication process. Our aim in this chapter is to discuss how multiple imagery, multiple image sources, and multiple production sites contribute to journalistic witnessing processes. Witnessing refers to the symbolic relations between home audiences and people and events in the war zone, as provided by still photography or live footage (also see Chapter 1). In war and conflict, witnessing

DOI: 10.4324/9781003478072-2

has always been a core journalistic activity, both verbally and visually. The photographic evidence and the ability of photography to document emotions, civil, and military life and situated physical landscapes give legitimacy to a (partial) truth claim: "I was there, I saw it, it happened". Metaphorically, witnessing serves as a bridge between here and there, us and them.

The empirical material is drawn from our mapping of three periods during the war (see Chapter 1 for details). We look at visual witnessing accounts from the first two weeks after the invasion (24 February–9 March 2022) from the perspective of networks and flows (Henning 2018), how visibility (Chouliaraki & Stolic 2017; Frosh 2011; Somerstein 2020) affects witnessing in the tragedies of Bucha and Borodyanka discovered in April 2022, and finally how time generates witnessing patterns in the form of visual tropes and figures (Zarzycka & Kleppe 2013) by looking at the visual commemoration of a year at war in published materials from February 2023.

Witnessing, networks, and flows

For an image to reach the public, it has to pass through a network consisting of several human and non-human actors. The human actors are all *image brokers* (Gürsel 2016) in one way or the other. Photographers, both amateur and professionals (in-house and agency), decide what images they capture and what images they file (or, if amateur, what image to upload on social media). Photo editors decide what image to use or possibly refer to verification specialists. Some photo editors are specialized but, as Gürsel predicted in 2016 (p. 281), due to cutbacks in the industry it is just as common to have journalists decide for themselves what image to use in a story. As one informant told us: "We have a hundred photo editors at our outlet. The only thing they know [about visual meaning-making processes] is that they need a face to illustrate their story". Editors are also image brokers, in the sense that they commission certain stories or endorse certain ideas, influencing what photographers and journalists may look for. Finally, we would also include different levels of designers, as they influence or operate the layout principles within which the images perform.

The non-human actors are the technical devices that produce and disseminate images and provide them with metadata that facilitate their potential flow through the networks. These are the handheld cameras, mobile phones, satellites, and drones that capture the images, and the digital transmission systems, archival systems, and publication systems through which they pass.

All actors contribute to the meaning-making processes in different ways, thus complicating the idea of journalistic witnessing (our main concern in this chapter) as unilinear and intended. If we add the decoding capacities of the public/s (Hall 2009), it becomes difficult to draw conclusions about the effects of witnessing. What we can do, however, is to investigate some of the spatial and temporal conditions for visual meaning-making in journalistic systems and suggest how they work together and what they do. We will start each section in this chapter by examining the production conditions in the field and then move on to the site of publication.

Witnessing outbreak: time, space, and production in the field

At the outbreak of the invasion, Scandinavian teams were located in Kyiv, Kharkiv, and Kramatorsk or at the Polish/Ukrainian border. Even if the invasion was anticipated, curfews, blackouts, and a general confusion and Ukrainian suspicion of foreigners being Russian spies made it difficult to work (see Chapter 3). Some teams were told by their media outlets to evacuate and others had little mobility. Most outlets compensated by sending teams to Romania, Poland, and Georgia to cover refugee stories or neighboring countries' point of view. The Norwegian media also sent teams to the Norwegian/Russian border. The teams in the field produced on average 1–2 stories a day, as opposed to an average of 28 daily news stories in the paper editions and 90 news stories in the web editions during the first week and 23 news stories in the paper editions and 73 news stories in the web editions in the second week.[1] The bulk of imagery thus originated from other sources, such as social-media entries and international news agencies. Among the agency photographers, many were Ukrainian nationals, but even agency material often originated from third-party sources, thus stressing the urgent need for verification tools (this will be further discussed in Chapter 4).

With mobile technology, real-time documentation of crises and dramatic events is no longer exclusive for photojournalists (Andén-Papadopoulos & Pantti 2013). Citizen witnessing has the advantage of being part of the action, while photojournalists tend to arrive later at the scene. Accordingly, the first days of the invasion were dominated by live footage showing explosions, Russian tanks crushing civilian cars, cars leaving the Ukrainian capital Kyiv, etc. Some imagery originated from military sources, but most were civilian testimonies uploaded onto social-media platforms. The videos were generally edited into short, gif-like footage, where some 10–20 seconds of an event plays as a loop. In the published stories, source attribution was often limited to the social-media platform they were harvested from, not specific individuals.

For professional photojournalists or multiskilled reporters, capturing a photograph is not particularly time-consuming. The real work is knowing where to go, procuring transport and permissions, considering safety aspects, getting access to relevant sites, and finding and finally photographing relevant sources. All Scandinavian teams in our sample relied on fixers to be able to get around, and at the frontlines they were also dependent upon the goodwill of the Ukrainian armed forces (see Chapter 3 for further discussion). The physical sites thus define what can and cannot be photographed. The published images, as well as our interviews, confirm that photojournalists only had access to the Ukrainian side of the war. In the first few weeks, the frontlines were mostly covered by international agency photographers, while the Scandinavian teams had a stronger coverage of refugees and the human consequences of the invasion. Russian troops were mostly covered by satellite images showing columns of tanks moving across the Ukrainian landscape or the occasional dead bodies of Russian soldiers. Several news outlets in our sample had correspondents in Russia at the outbreak of war, but some had to leave and the few who remained had little opportunity to do field reporting. Their contributions are thus most commonly found in the commentary/analysis sections.

We will discuss questions related to pro-Ukrainian bias in Chapter 3, but from a witnessing point of view the lack of access to Russian sources contributed to the dehumanization of Russian soldiers as faceless and interchangeable. A David versus Goliath theme in the journalistic reporting was visually reinforced by the ample display of Ukrainian civilians fleeing for safety, preparing Molotov cocktails, or training to use firearms to protect themselves, while the Russians were represented by tanks, unidentifiable bodies, and, as we shall see in the section on Bucha, the traces of violence and destruction they left behind.

The intimacy and relatability of a photograph is often a product of the time spent in the field as well as the type of assignment the photographer is on. According to a freelance photojournalist in our interview sample who has worked for a variety of news media, there is usually not enough time in the field: "What I love about freelancing is that it gives me the opportunity to stay as long as I would like. Spending time with people makes them trust you more, and this becomes visible because they will let their guard down and behave more naturally and less tense". This photojournalist, who also has experience as an agency photographer, explained that the agencies favor different images than the individual news outlets:

> When I do an assignment for a specific media outlet, it is all about specific stories, getting close to people and showing presence. Or it could be to show some link to the audience at home. But for the agencies, when I work for them, it is more about creating general stories, and to record the news events […]. If there is time, you can do other stuff but it has to be rather generic and adaptable.

Presence in the field is thus vital to witnessing, but it does not guarantee cultural, political, or societal understanding of an event or a community. Journalistic presence implies a certain intimacy in relation to the sources, but in real life this is not always the case. A live stand-up may be far from the action and the people involved, even if the reporter is visibly present in the country. A news story may have relevant or less relevant sources, relative to the reporter's knowledge, access, and journalistic skills. Breaking news images may need cultural or political translation to make sense to the home audiences, and there is often not enough time to provide sufficient contextual information.

Agency material from the war in Ukraine often did not identify the people in the images, which is understandable from a safety perspective. Yet, nameless people will often be perceived as generic examples rather than individual persons with unique stories. In-house coverage from the field reflects a higher degree of intimacy in the witnessing mode, in particular in reportage. Single images run the same risk of generic exemplification as agency images (Caple 2019).

Witnessing outbreak from home

War reporting from the home desk has other temporal and spatial challenges than working in the field. Journalists on the foreign desk generally have better prerequisites for understanding a war theater than generalists, and most outlets in our sample had in-house staff who had followed the events in Ukraine since the Maidan uprising in 2013 and the Russian annexation of Crimea in 2014. Most of the news outlets in our sample had the foreign desk leading the way but, as the war in Ukraine was perceived as a conflict with consequences transcending Ukrainian borders, a great number of generalists also covered the events.

As noted above, the amount of news stories produced from the home desks was the most extensive. Almost everything from and about Ukraine was considered breaking news and published at a rapid pace. The fastest of all were the super-rapid news-feed entries, at the outbreak of war almost on a minute-by-minute basis. The news feeds in our sample were generally between 20 and 100 words and often based on agency-produced statements from politicians or briefings from the war theater. This coverage manifests and concretizes the news stream available to the media outlets, as there was limited original reporting and editing involved. All available news was pushed onto the public, and some of these bits and pieces were reused and assembled into more developed news stories later in the day. Several of the news bits turned out to be of limited significance, but the amount and pulse in the news-feed coverage speaks to the feeling of immediate crisis and to the political frenzy it inspired, in Scandinavia as well as other European countries, the UN headquarter, NATO, and elsewhere.

Visually, the news feeds are the least interesting. In most cases, they were published with no image at all, and when images were used, they were mainly illustrations. By illustration we mean that they underline or double aspects of the textual message (van Leeuwen 2020, p. 3) often in a generic manner found to be increasing in modern news coverage (Fabregat 2013; Vobič & Trivundža 2015). Most commonly the news-feed imagery would depict politicians, with little inherent news value as they basically show what the politician looks like. This does not imply that all images in news feeds are redundant. In the morning of 24 February, when Putin on Russian television declared his approval of a "special military operation" in Eastern Ukraine, several outlets pushed a screenshot of the Russian president at his desk during the declaration, with Russian subtitles. In this case, the image complemented the text and added news value. Variations of this freeze frame were among the most downloaded images by customers of the Swedish news agency TT and its Norwegian equivalent NTB. As such it can be said to have served as a *transitional object* (Mitchell 2007, p. 75) while waiting for visual documentation from the field.

When reporting from the home desk, the sources are distant and visual choices often depend on finding something suitable to illustrate a story. As noted above, journalistic field reports were scarce at the beginning of the war, but social media provided an opportunity to create a different kind of proximity to the ongoing events. Directly after the invasion, social media were a much-used proxy for journalistic witnessing. There are two main categories in our material: The first (also mentioned above) contained live footage showing war actions, such as explosions and Russian tanks. They were mainly displayed online as live footage, but sometimes a media outlet would make a still image from a news gif and publish in their paper editions. The gifs were seldom people-centered but usually focused on events. They presented live drama and were often emotional, but the human emotions were typically communicated through sound (outbursts, stressed voices) rather than image.

The other category contains social-media postings from Ukrainian influencers or local celebrities, mostly young women. They were sometimes used illustratively, yet several became news stories in their own right, presenting young women who communicated that their world had been turned upside down. Many of these women wanted to contribute to the fight, either by learning how to handle guns or by way of informing the world (their social-media followers) about the Ukrainian plight. Visually, most of these entries were highly theatrical and staged. The influencers posed with immaculate makeup, shiny hair, and Mona Lisa half-smiles, often in stark contrast to their verbal messages about being angry, afraid, and ready to fight. In these examples, the text carried the emotional testimonies, while the images seemed remote and detached. However, as noted by Mortensen & Pantti (2023, p. 10), such "war influencers" have been highly effective advocates on their own social-media sites narrating everyday trauma in non-traditional ways.

Some outlets engaged Ukrainian civilians to report on their daily lives under siege, as a supplement to other modes of reporting. Visually, this represented a different form of testimonial witnessing than that of the influencers. In one example, from the Norwegian tabloid *Dagbladet*, a Kyiv-based individual produced a war diary complemented by private photos. The visual material mostly consisted of selfies, basically documenting state of mind, not actions of war. In the photographs, the diary writer often appeared worried, smoking, and with a tired look on his face. He sometimes contributed details of daily life, like his mother knitting when she could not sleep. His images were not of high professional quality, and their visual value was in the way they display emotional affect.

Visual relations in online and print publications

Visual relations between home audiences and the war site are highly contextual and depend not only on the image content itself but on several factors related to publication, such as the publicizing media outlet's orientation and tradition, journalistic genre, production pace, production site, narrational mode, and visual mode.

In a journalistic setting, the image never stands alone, even though individual images often are separated from their original context. The meaning-making processes in a newspaper spread or on a website are complex and depend on the interplay between image, text, and design. Mitchell (2002) emphasizes the ability of images to create text and of text to create images, while Hagan (2023, 2007) stresses that the two modalities are fundamentally different, both structurally, experientially, and sensorially. Yet they work together as complementary meaning-producers, tied together by layout and design (Hagan 2023, 2007). In the words of Hagan, text and image "collaborate as equals to offer claims linked to reasons or proof in messages that would significantly change if one of the modalities were altered or removed" (Hagan, 2023, p. 3). They work together through intricate processes of grouping and bridging that are beyond the scope of this study.

In day-to-day news production, the online platform is the most rapid and dynamic. Online news stories are not final in the same way as newspaper stories but subject to potentially endless rectifications and updates, both textually and visually. The paper editions usually offer a selection of the digital content but with a time lag. More importantly for our purpose, they visualize the stories differently. This affects the narrational form in significant ways.

Online editions

Online news configurations often involve what Hagan (2007, p. 53) calls an *interplay in sequence* between image and text, where the public's access to the material is guided by a main narrative that develops as one reads. Live footage and image carousels represent stories within the story that the onlooker is free to digest or drop. Such online news stories operate as a menu offering different levels of depth and detail. One example is retrieved from *VG* on 25 February 2022, the day after the invasion. A journalist/photographer team had visited a military post at the border between Ukraine, Russia, and Belarus, waiting to be attacked. The story opens with a lead image showing two armed Ukrainian soldiers walking in a snow-covered forest. They are well camouflaged and could easily be confused with trees or brush if not for their movements. We don't meet their eyes, and they are presented more as typecast soldiers than individual human beings. The image thus conveys a condensed visual message of patriotism. Further down, however, we are introduced to leading characters, background, overviews, and details. The humanity of the soldiers is deepened by reportage images of three male soldiers in casual conversation, a portrait of a female frontier guard posing in profile in a contemplating way, a brief live interview with a female military officer, a brief stand-up explaining where the reporter team is, and why. Finally, the story is broadened by an interview with an elderly civilian couple living in the area, expressing their disbelief in what is about to happen among what they call "brother nations".

Online feature stories were sometimes presented as "scrollytelling" (Seyser & Zeiller 2018), a visual storytelling technique where content appears or changes as users scroll up or down a page. Scrollytelling has a certain "filmic" quality (Barthes 1977, p. 65) as they are visually driven, and an image may fill the screen in its entirety. Moving layers of text are often superimposed onto the images and anchor the visual meaning.

One example of a visually driven reportage is retrieved from *Aftenposten* on 6 March, during the second week after the invasion. This is one among several stories we found focusing on fleeing civilians and refugees crossing borders. In the story, titled "The escape from Kyiv," a reporter/photojournalist-team joins a train from Kyiv to Bucharest scheduled to leave after a 36-hour curfew. The opening image shows a man and a group of five children crossing the railway tracks. The man is carrying a large suitcase in one hand and with the other he steadies a young girl balancing on his shoulders. The text underneath explains the context, followed by a scrollytelling section of three full-screen photographs documenting the massive amount of people scurrying over the railway tracks, onto the platforms, and into the train. The reporter team gets onboard the train and, in smaller pictures intersected by text, we are presented with several civilian narratives: the young couple with no definite destination, the elderly woman leaving Kyiv after 59 years, and the Indian exchange students who wish to go home. The story ends in a refugee shelter in Romania, where the refugees are met by smiling and empathic local volunteers.

Print editions

In print editions, we often find what Hagan (2007, p. 53) calls *interplay in parallel* between image and text. The public is free to enter the story where they wish, but the images are grouped together for narrational purposes. There are several variants of parallel interplay. If we look at the paper version of the story mentioned above, "The escape from Kyiv," the visual presentation is much simpler. The lead image is the same: the man and five children on the train rails. The picture is positioned as the visual centerpiece on the two-page spread and covers almost half of the available space in width and two thirds in height. Underneath is one of the images from the train, a portrait of the old woman who had to leave Kyiv after 59 years. The smaller picture covers two columns and is balanced with a quote on the left side. The layout is clean and minimal and, contrary to the online version, the layout signals that this is news, not a feature story. Even if the picture is big, the text looks massive, and while the two modalities complement each other, they are not integrated.

As mentioned above, we find few single image entries in our sample; however, configurations with one leading image and one or two smaller ones are quite common. *Aftenposten* is a subscription outlet (like the Swedish *Dagens Nyheter* and *Svenska Dagbladet*), and as such more muted in its presentation than the tabloids. In the tabloid paper editions, the variety of image/text configurations is greater and aesthetically more focused on contrast than harmony (Evensen & Simonsen 2019). One example is a background story from *VG* on 26 February called "The Russian invasion". In this story, the map of Ukraine covers an entire two-page spread. Independent Ukraine, occupied Crimea, separatist-controlled Donbas, and Ukrainian-controlled Donbas are colored in different shades of red (signaling occupation) and green (signaling independence). Ongoing Russian attacks are marked on the map with small orange explosion symbols, and images from the field are linked to each explosion. In total there are 11 photographs superimposed on the map, all positioned at the fringes of the Ukrainian border on the map. There are very few people in the images and no portraits. Ukrainian society is visualized by buildings, cars, tanks, and military equipment. The text is minimal and, apart from the explanatory title, it consists only of captions. All the images originate from international agencies. This story is visually driven, highly dramatic with stark contrasts between the elements. It is chaotic in the sense that several things are going on simultaneously on the news spread, yet pedagogically simple. The spread shows the political outline of Ukraine, where the Russians are attacking, and excerpts of the destruction following the attacks.

A third variant, from another Norwegian tabloid, published by *Dagbladet* on 2 March, shows a more conceptual approach. The story anticipates Russian brutality at war, with reference to the destruction of the Chechen capital Grozny in 1999–2000. All the sources are Norwegian military experts and NGO representatives, and all the images are agency material. In a three-page spread in the paper edition, the lead image shows two Russian soldiers recently killed in the streets of Kharkiv. Underneath is an archival image from Grozny, which serves as a visual reminder of Russian brutality as something to be expected. Two smaller pictures to the right show Ukrainian vehicles destroyed by Russian troops a few days earlier and smoke rising from a Russian attack on the TV tower in Kyiv. On the third page a satellite image documents Russian military vehicles approaching Kyiv, and superimposed on this image is a map showing ongoing Russian attacks along the Ukrainian border. Underneath is a picture of civilians in Kyiv preparing Molotov cocktails in the street. Finally, there is a small headshot of the Norwegian head of defense, as he is interviewed in the story. All the images are grouped together at the top of the page, filling approximately two thirds of the pages. The configuration signals that the visual content tells a story of its own. While the text anticipates a possibly brutal future, based on historic events in Grozny, the images show the brutality "here and now" in an almost cartoonish manner. Each element contributes to a plot documenting heroes and villains in the present while simultaneously anticipating an even darker future.

Summary: random and deliberate coverage

The configurational patterns above relate to production pace, genre, publication modality, and, most significantly, whether a news story is produced from the home desk or from the field. This difference matters because news production from home is distant from the action and likely to be filtered through domestic concerns, world views, and preconceptions (Eide & Simonsen 2008). Images are used not only to document or illustrate but also to create an illusion of presence. News from the field is closer to the realities on the ground. To return to our two examples from the field above (the *VG* report from the Ukrainian border and the *Aftenposten* story about refugees), we meet real people with names and individual background stories. This makes them more relatable, even if the meetings are fleeting. In the stories produced from home (the anticipatory story from *Dagbladet* and the mapping of ongoing Russian attacks in *VG*), there are few human beings, all images originate from news agencies, nobody has names or personal stories, and they appear remote and replaceable.

Based on examples like these, we have identified two modes of operation that we find significant for understanding how visuals perform in multimodal journalism. We have labeled them "random" and "intentional" coverage, based on the following characteristics:

Random coverage refers to how visual media professionals, mostly on the home desks, operate image flows provided by international news agencies, including satellite images. Random coverage occurs when news professionals depend on the external news flow and search the news agencies' image feeds to select photographs that can illustrate or document stories, in particular breaking news. The term "random" is chosen because the influx of images to choose from is vast, and there is usually limited time for comparisons and deliberations. The selection is dependent upon what the feed can offer when the search is being conducted, and this temporal dimension makes the selection somewhat arbitrary. The indexicality, understood as the bi-modal link between text and image, is often weakened because of the conceptual (symbolic) nature of illustrative images.

Deliberate coverage refers to visual stories initiated by the news outlets themselves or their representatives in the field. Deliberate coverage refers to what traditionally has been conceptualized as photojournalism or visually driven news narratives with an identifiable "author". Photojournalistic storytelling implies a strong text/image connection that secures the reliability of the photographic indexical value (also see Chapters 1 and 4).

These categories are ideal types that need constant contextualization, but they are useful for discussing how images work in different ways to bridge the gap between a home audience and the war theater or a war-affected society. It should be noted that the dichotomy does not apply to the distinction between agency and in-house visuals in a 1:1 manner. In-house produced photographs may contribute to random coverage in the same way as agency images when

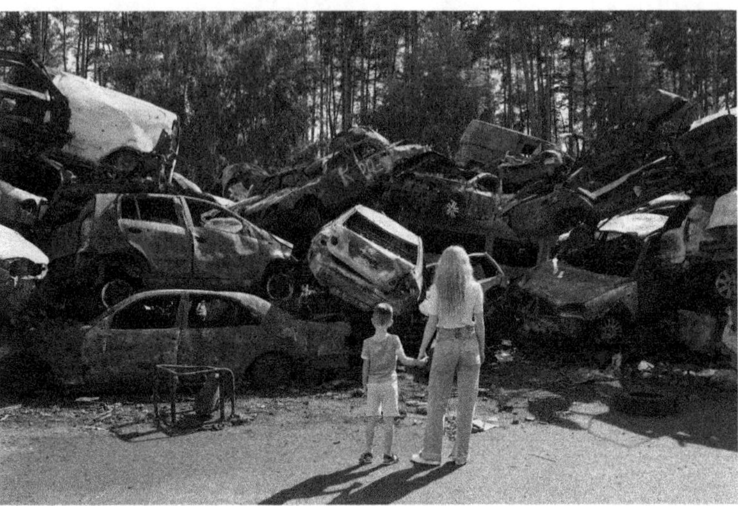

Figure 2.1 Bucha in June 2022. Three months after the massacres, life continues. Photo by Kyrre Lien, VG. Reproduced with permission.

used as illustrations, while deliberate coverage may include conscious use of agency material. One example of the latter is a story in *Aftenposten* on 7 March about Ukrainian men who stayed to fight while their female relatives left the country. This story is called "The men who must stay behind" and it is visualized by a mix of agency images and private images. The lead image is by agency photographer, Emilio Morenatti (AP), and represents a man with visible tears in his eyes as he waves goodbye to a train leaving the platform. The main textual source is a Norwegian researcher reflecting on Ukraine's mobilization strategy, and the story proceeds by presenting five Ukrainian men, two sales representatives, a farmer, and a drama teacher who are now transitioning to soldiers. The fifth man is a student who managed to flee to Romania before the general mobilization of Ukrainian men. The interviews are visualized by private images, selfies, and details like a table where one of the men stores weapon and ammunition or a broken window. They are mixed with more general agency images which are less intimate but provide context. None of the images are generated by in-house photographers, yet the story comes across as intimate and relatable with deliberately selected imagery.

Witnessing atrocities: the cases of Bucha and Borodyanka

From the end of March 2022, a month after the invasion, Ukrainian forces managed to regain the Russian-occupied cities surrounding the capital Kyiv.

Irpin, a city/community, on the Western outskirts of Kyiv was recaptured on 28 March after heavy fighting, and the media were filled with accounts of violence, destruction, and suffering. In April, accounts of Russian atrocities in the small city of Bucha, a little further to the west, started to spread, and on 3 April, a team from the Norwegian public broadcaster NRK was among the first to document what the Russian troops had left behind. Piggybacking on Ukrainian troops, the Scandinavians, and other international teams filmed and photographed bodies of dead civilians in the streets of Bucha. Several had been there for days or weeks, some were shot while carrying groceries, and some while riding a bike or taking the dog for a walk. The images sent shock waves through the international community, and the shock deepened when mass graves were discovered a few days later.

In retrospect, it appears that almost 500 people were killed in Bucha, several of them tortured and burned. Young girls and women were raped. Ukraine asked the International Criminal Court to investigate the killings as war crimes or crimes against humanity. Russian authorities, on the other hand, claimed that the images were staged and that the bodies in the streets were actors.

Most outlets in our sample had teams in Bucha, arriving a couple of days after the city was opened. Contrary to the outbreak period, where agency material and in-house Scandinavian teams did complementary reporting (agencies focusing on the front lines and in-house teams on civilian life and refugees), the difference between agency material and in-house material is less apparent in Bucha. All visual reporters largely repeated each other, photographing the same bodies and the same body parts (hands and feet) emerging from the mass graves. The major difference in the visual accounts was that the Scandinavian teams interviewed, photographed, and named more and other local witnesses, thus deepening the overall story, anchoring the truth claims of the initial reports. Teams from some of the Scandinavian outlets returned to Bucha and other towns later in April to cover the excavation and examination of mass graves. One team even returned in June to see how people were coping and how the city returned to life. Most media also published satellite imagery documenting the timeline of the atrocities for forensic purposes and to rebuff the Russian claims that the images were staged.

On 7 April, Volodymyr Zelenskyy claimed that another small city, Borodyanka, situated further to the west, had suffered a similar and possibly worse fate than Bucha. The city was bombed to pieces in the beginning of March during the Russian attempt to capture Kyiv. Hundreds of people were trapped and died in the rubble. On their way back, the Russian troops passed through the almost deserted Borodyanka again, placing landmines. The total number of casualties is not clear, but according to CBC on 3 March 2023, almost 200 bodies remained unidentified, while 280 people were listed as missing.[2] Also in this city, reports were made of murder, torture, and beatings of civilians. In one Norwegian story, from *VG* on 6 April, a woman poses beside a ditch in her garden, claiming that the Russians had prepared it as a mass grave.

From a witnessing perspective, there are several things to be noted from the coverage of these atrocities. First, the brutality in Bucha seems to have pushed the ethical boundaries regarding visualizing war crimes, an assessment that was confirmed in interviews with editors (see Chapter 3). Scandinavian media are generally restrictive when it comes to publishing explicit images of violence (Nilsson 2019), but Bucha was a rare case of direct access to a massive crime scene. Russian brutality against civilians was perceived as a strategic weapon, and documenting this aspect of their conduct transcended the "normal" coverage of human suffering at war (Nilsson 2022). In addition to the bodies themselves, scattered in the streets or in backyards, the visual coverage showed Ukrainian soldiers searching for booby traps under dead bodies, civilians carrying bodies away from the streets and body counts at the edge of the mass graves.

In our analyses of all coverage about Bucha in the first week of April, we found several instances where editors reflected on their decisions to publish explicit imagery, such as the subscription-based daily *Dagens Nyheter* running a full-page cover photo in the 4 April print edition showing dead bodies, their faces blotted. This departure from the paper's policy not to show images of dead and wounded victims was accompanied by an article from a top editor explaining their decision to publish. We found other similar examples where editors shared their deliberations with readers as well as discussed the ethics and contributions of photojournalism as a witness. Scholarship on crisis coverage has identified this as a strategy for the news media to position themselves as ethical in moments when controversial images or, the reverse, decisions to withhold visuals rise in the public debate about photography and ethics (e.g. Mortensen et al. 2017). These issues are further discussed in Chapter 3.

A second point is how the visibility of war crimes affects collective remembrance. Visibility is related to what can be seen (and photographed) and also to what photographers look for or, in our context, what they have access to (see Chapter 3 for further discussion). While the atrocities in Bucha became public to an unusual degree, with the international news media as a first-hand witness, the coverage of Borodyanka's fate is more common. Borodyanka was also visited by several teams in our sample, and the stories from the city were strong. Visually, however, the coverage was dominated by destroyed buildings, not dead bodies.

As noted by several scholars (Chouliaraki & Stolic 2017; Frosh 2011; Somerstein 2020), being visible invokes "being human". Though the suffering of others is often not fully relatable to distant onlookers, visibility still ensures that it is at least noticed (Frosh 2011). Bucha is a rare case in this respect as it was covered by multiple media outlets, while the events were still visibly fresh. Although the individual names from Bucha may be forgotten by most, the visual impact of the killings and the mistreatment of the dead bodies left a mark that still resonates in Scandinavian news as a symbol of Russian brutality. While the number of casualties in Borodyanka was also substantial, their fate seems to have blended into the general story about civilian suffering in Ukraine.

The figure below shows the frequency of stories mentioning Bucha (the upper curve) and Borodyanka (the lower curve) in all outlets in our sample. It demonstrates the massive breaking news interest in April 2022, followed by a sharp decline. Bucha, however, reappears in the material, mostly in connection to other stories about Russian violence against civilians, such as the discovery of the mass graves in Izium in September 2022. The mention of Borodyanka is significantly smaller and has mostly disappeared. In relation to commemorative stories on the one-year mark of the invasion, Bucha and Borodyanka are both referred to, but again with a marked difference in scope. At the two-year mark, Bucha is still an active reference point, while Borodyanka has disappeared.

As noted by Zelizer, journalism contributes to collective memory work in various ways. According to her, journalism and journalists "are an unobvious but fertile site of memory, and their status as memory agents needs to be better understood" (Zelizer 2008, p. 81). Journalists need history to "position its recounting of public events in context", which in many ways is what we see happening when Bucha is recurrently brought to the attention in analysis and commemorative, summarizing journalistic stories. Journalism is also a source for historians and others who shape accounts about former events, as the news media "provide one of the most public drafts of the past" (ibid, p.79).

At the core of journalistic memory work, photojournalistic images serve as "lieux de memoire" for both individual actors and collectives. Images that are circulated widely sometimes develop iconic status because they are used as complex memory containers in the intersection between politics, public art, and social life (Hariman & Lucaites 2007). In the digital world, individual photographs are less likely to acquire status as popular icons (e.g. the naked girl running from napalm during the Vietnam war in 1972, or the individual

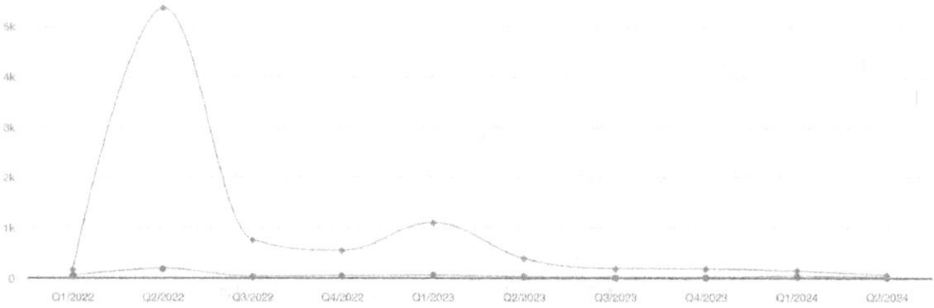

Figure 2.2 Frequency differences in the coverage of Bucha and Borodyanka in Norwegian and Swedish media.

standing in front of a Chinese tank during the Tiananmen Square uprising in 1989). As pointed out by Merrill: "Through virality, collective memory [...] becomes influenced by a rapid turnover of content (including photos) that temporarily reaches the forefront of public attention" (Merrill 2023, p. 136). Yet, even if the single image seldom gains mnemonic longevity, visual records from salient events, such as Bucha, may take on symbolic status as a group. In so doing, they undergo some of the same processes as iconic photographs did in the past, where symbolism overrides the indexicality of the images (Hariman & Lucaites 2007). Bucha seems to have the potential of becoming a metonym for all Russian violence in Ukraine, more than a specific site with a specific experience.

Witnessing through tropes and conventions: commemorating the invasion

Commemorative stories reflect editorial memory work as they project the events, scenes, and single images the news outlet wishes to highlight as memorable. To explore this, we analyzed commemorative stories from 24 February 2023, the one-year mark of the invasion, focusing on how time generates witnessing patterns in the form of visual tropes and figures. As the symbolic value of imagery develops with time, we conclude the section by discussing these stories in relation to visual tropes found in our materials throughout the year.

Tropes are symbolic visual figures articulating certain conventions, be it in literature, the arts, or, in our case, photojournalism. Common visual figures in war photography include the male soldier, the grieving woman, the innocence of children, and the refugee as either victim or threat (e.g. Chouliaraki & Stolic 2017). While the figures are representations of real people, a depiction relying on clichéd tropes may reproduce preconceptions rather than convey new information (see Chapter 1; Choularaki & Stolic 2017). According to Newton, visual tropes are "ideologically pre-structured, they function as mental and emotional templates; they do not document or bear witness, but rather symbolically represent marketable concepts" (Newton 2008, cited in Zarzycka & Kleppe 2013, p. 980).

For our analysis we selected one story from each news outlet in our sample published in February 2023 in the online edition, as these publish the most images. Most Norwegian media presented a mix of agency and in-house photos, while *Dagbladet* published mostly agency material and *Aftenposten* only in-house. Similarly, among the Swedish outlets, there was a mix of news agency, social media, and in-house visuals among the outlets. The public-service outlets in both countries had a day-long television special on 24 February, which may have resulted in fewer posts on their digital sites. We identified one visually driven svt.se story, to be discussed below.

2024-11-14 10:21 SvD '2022-03-08 - sida 1

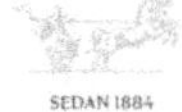

Tisdag 8 mars 2022

SEDAN 1884

ÅRETS DAGSTIDNING

SVENSKA DAGBLADET

Elaf Ali: Det är dags att Sveriges feminister slutar att blunda för hedersförtrycket och börjar engagera sig för alla kvinnor.

Kultur | Sid 23

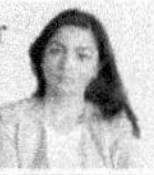

S-ministrar: Vi måste göra upp med unkna könsroller som gör kvinnor till fattigpensionärer

Debatt | Sid 4

Kampvilja och osande raseri, tårar och desperation, skratt och kramar. Kvällen tillsammans med den ukrainska familjen Semenuik och deras vänner blir en känslomässig berg- och dalbana. Foto: Staffan Löwstedt

En sista måltid – sedan inleds flykten från Ukraina

Familjen och vännerna äter tillsammans innan alla sprids över världen. SvD är med under sista kvällen bland Ukrainas berg.

Tomas Lundin: Hjälpte väst till att skapa en aggressor när Sovjetunionen föll?

Svenskarnas stöd för Nato har ökat med tio procentenheter – på en vecka.

Oljepriset kan stiga till 185 dollar per fat om USA stoppar rysk olja, tror expert.

Nyheter | Sid 6–15, Kultur | Sid 20, Näringsliv | Sid 4–9

Om det går lätt att plugga – då gör du nog fel

Lärande fungerar ungefär på samma sätt som styrketräning – ju mer vi sliter när vi pluggar till ett prov, desto mer verkar vi lära oss. Jobbigt i stunden – men nyttigt på sikt. Ungefär som broccoli, säger Nate Kornell, professor i kognitiv psykologi, i serien "Hjärnan och lärandet".

Livet | Sid 20–21

Jag gillar inte "sälj grej med tjej"-reklam som vi ser hela tiden.

Influencerstjärnan Therese Lindgren **om att verka för ett hållbart samhälle och motverka sexistisk reklam.**

Näringsliv | Sid 10–11

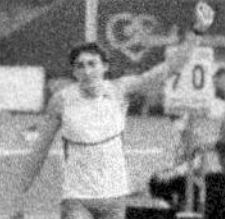

Armand Duplantis. Foto: Pedja Milosavljevic Bildbyrån

Världsrekord för Armand Duplantis

På måndagen hoppade Armand Duplantis 6,19 meter i Belgrad och 22-åringen har därmed slagit sitt eget världsrekord i stavhopp. "Äntligen, var min första reaktion", säger Duplantis.

Sport | Sid 24–25

KONTAKTA SvD www.SvD.se

about:blank 1/1

Figure 2.3 "A final meal-before starting the flight from Ukraine," one of several in-house reportages by the outlets in the early part of the invasion. Photo by Staffan Löwstedt, *Svenska Dagbladet*. Reproduced with permission from *Svenska Dagbladet*, and from Bildbyrån for the sports picture.

The stories share some commonalities. Apart from the NRK, who published a commentary supplemented by visual illustrations on their online site, all Norwegian stories discussed here are visually driven. They all summarize the year more or less chronologically, and they all accentuate Ukrainian sacrifice and heroism. Only one of the Swedish stories (*Svenska Dagbladet*) summarizes the entire year visually, while *Dagens Nyheter* and *SVT* focus on personal stories to portray the impact of the war on the people of Ukraine and *Expressen* and *Aftonbladet* commemorate the beginning of the invasion. Despite these contrasts in topic, the outlets in both countries adopted narrational modes falling into two main categories: *military* and *civilian* focus.

Military focus

VG ("The day that changed the world") opens with a social-media video from 24 February 2022 and presents the events in chapters, underlining Russian brutality in Bucha and Mariupol and military failures in the attempt to conquer Kyiv, Kharkiv, and Kherson. The story also includes a chapter on the exploded gas pipeline in the Baltic Sea, Russia's attacks on Ukrainian infrastructure, in particular power plants, and finally an overview of the military obstacles ahead. Visually the story echoes the imagery available in the different phases of the war: social-media videos from the first days and in-house material from Bucha, Kharkiv, and Kherson supplemented with agency material and satellite imagery.

Dagbladet ("The decisive battles of the war") also concentrated on the military aspects of the war and only 4 out of 30 images focused on civilians in the story. There are also three images of Putin and two of Zelenskyy. Otherwise, the visual story comes across as haphazard as most images were without byline, and in several cases the location was not clear.

Expressen ("The historic pictures: the first day of the invasion of Ukraine,") published a video/tv-broadcast segment mixing in-house materials with social-media content and reporting by international agencies. The piece opens with the newspaper's team in Ukraine reporting from Kramatorsk about the first Russian attacks hitting the city. Social-media visuals are then interspersed throughout the video, showing plumes of smoke in pre-dawn images shot from apartment windows. Clips from CNN reports follow, with video showing Russian troops crossing into Ukraine from Belarus. Putin appears in a video clip declaring the start of "the special operations", followed by condemnations by international political leaders. The piece commemorates the uncertainty and threat of the first day, inviting readers to re-experience it.

Aftonbladet ("The Russian invasion of Ukraine: One year later") published an in-house produced, aesthetically sophisticated scrollytelling story narrated through full-screen photos, video, aerial shots, maps, and graphics as well as explanatory text, with visual sources including agency, satellite visuals, and staff. Commemorating the Battle of Kyiv (from 24 February through the liberation of Bucha), the piece opens with a subtitle framing the story as a strategic failure of an incompetent Russian military. Visually, the piece starts with Ukrainian soldiers, citizens evacuating on jammed highways, and by train, followed by the stalled advance of Russian tanks and satellite visuals and maps showing the operation, ending with atrocities committed by the Russian forces, in images of exhumation of mass graves and the reburial of the victims of Bucha.

Civilian focus

TV 2 ("The cost of war") opens with a live closeup from a graveyard in Dnipro. The graves are fresh, and they are numerous. Closing in on one of them provides the viewer with a face and a name before we are introduced to the fallen soldier's father and family. From the Dnipro case, the story zooms out to present an overview of the number of civilian casualties in all of Ukraine. It then zooms in on the atrocities in Bucha and Borodyanka (illustrated by dead bodies in Bucha and destroyed buildings in Chernihiv and Borodyanka). Visually, the story ends with an image of Ukrainian soldiers in Kherson with their backs to the camera. One of them suffers from a head wound covered by a bandage, and he is supported by a colleague. Still, the image signals hope in this context. The soldiers have suffered hardship, but Kherson was won, and they stumble on. The timeline of major events over the year is not presented until the last image, in white letters and red markers against a black background.

Aftenposten ("One year since the invasion of Ukraine") also presented an almost exclusively civilian perspective, focusing on daily life from before and during the war. Through the lenses of *Aftenposten's* own photographers, we meet people preparing for the invasion, training with wooden guns, or singing draped in the Ukrainian flag. Then we follow the refugees, onto trains, crossing the border into Poland or seeking refuge in other Ukrainian cities, such as Lviv. This story gets progressively less chronological. We are faced with a multitude of perspectives, from people taking shelter in the metro or waiting endlessly at checkpoints to digging up mass graves in Izium. Unique to this story is that there are no images from Bucha, but two images from Russia – a nuclear missile being paraded in the streets of Moscow and a graveyard in Krasnodar where some 150 Russian soldiers have been buried.

Svenska Dagbladet ("They practice fooling death—the images from the war") published a story consisting of 19 images in a roughly chronological narrative of the year. Most images show civilians, with only four photographs of soldiers, among them a female sniper, and two images showing material destruction. The visual narrative moves from military preparedness—the opening photo showing new cadets trying on gas masks—to the human cost: evacuation, the mortally wounded woman at the Mariupol hospital, a village funeral, a bicyclist lying dead in the street of Bucha, and others.

The second half has a hopeful tone, with family reunions, street musicians, and, in the final image, a couple embracing on a dance floor. Zelenskyy, in the widely shown X (Twitter) image of his 4 April visit to Bucha, does not appear until the middle of the narrative. He is shown again towards the end in a statesmanlike posture as he walks up the steps of the presidential palace in Kyiv alongside visiting US president Joe Biden. The story contains two images that could be called iconic: the dead bicyclist in Bucha and the mortally wounded mother of Mariupol.

Dagens Nyheter ("You want to say the words aloud—that we will be together until the end") published a staff reportage focusing on a Ukrainian couple who joined the civil guard and got married right after the Russian invasion; their social-media posts from the wedding, with the uniformed bride wearing a veil, were widely published at the time. The *Dagens Nyheter* story includes 13 images, of which 2 are private/social-media images and the remaining by a *Dagens Nyheter* photographer. The reportage has a documentary, every-day focus with signs of war included overtly or subtly: the couple at home in their couch accompanied by their cat and dog, the pet carriers at the ready (in case of evacuation), a park with a statue protected by sandbags, commuters in a subway station sheltering during an air raid, and a mother at the grave of her son at a military cemetery.

In a personalized reportage, *SVT* ("Oleksander lost his whole family in Bucha when the Russians opened fire") invites viewers to meet Oleksander who survived a Russian ambush while his wife and two children died as they attempted to flee Bucha by car in March 2022. The widower recounts the experience while showing pictures of his family, his mother appearing in the background, both of them visibly emotional. The piece is in the TV-documentary style where viewers are invited to view and listen to his story without the reporter's questions or voice-over (the reporter is in the frame at times, at one point consoling the mother). The piece commemorates Oleksander's family, through his own recollection and visit to the grave, and collectively commemorates everyone who suffered in Bucha and elsewhere in Ukraine.

NRK ("A changed world") produced a piece that belongs to a category of its own in this context, a commentary by the foreign editor highlighting the gravity of the war yet stressing that Ukraine has defended itself better than expected. The commentary opens with an image of Putin one year ahead of the invasion, and, interestingly, the second image in the story is a portrait of the NRK foreign editor in front of the Kremlin. The images are mainly illustrative (an example of a destroyed building, an affected grave-faced boy, a seriously wounded soldier) but they also bring forward a somewhat wider perspective than the others e.g. visualizing protests elsewhere in Europe (Berlin) and Russia's relations with China (a handshake between a Chinese diplomat and Putin).

The one-year mark stories summarize events, and the images used can be said to have a deliberate mnemonic function: "This is what we remember, and what we think you should remember". As such they imply a first step in the transition processes towards acquiring symbolic status (such as Bucha and Borodyanka discussed previously in this chapter). We identified several common themes in the commemorative stories. In the stories with civilian focus, we noted personal narratives representing the Ukrainian people, a strategy commonly used in reportages, commemoration shown as a private as well as a public memory process that includes personal grief and narrating (re-telling the experience) trauma, and the Ukrainian people as the protagonist. The stories with a military focus visualized Russian war crimes and incompetence and Ukrainian suffering and resilience. The stories we examined showed both the valor and sacrifice of soldiers and the suffering and resilience of civilians, mostly but not exclusively women and children, the trauma of war, and life continuing despite the conflict.

Commemorative stories are a tool for news outlets to showcase their own work, which was the case in several of these stories, through reportages by their own teams (*Dagens Nyheter*, *SVT*, *VG*, *Aftenposten*, TV 2), and to showcase in-house produced interactive visualizations (*Aftonbladet*). This strategy could also explain why we didn't find iconic visuals in the material. In the Norwegian selection, only two images are used more than one time. One depicts Ukrainian soldiers getting ready for battle on a bridge in Kyiv, and the other is the famous image of a pregnant woman being evacuated from the maternity ward in a hospital in Mariupol, which was also used in two of the Swedish stories. This suggests that the news outlets didn't rely on so-called iconic visuals that were widely circulated at the time of original publication in 2022. The commemorative stories also reflect variations of common conflict tropes found in the overall coverage (to be discussed below), such as heroism embodied by soldiers, suffering embodied by civilian women and refugees embodied as victims. Interestingly, refugees in our material run counter to the binary visualization of refugees as either victim or threat which is common in other conflicts and wars (Chouliaraki & Stolic 2017, p. 1164). For instance, in the Swedish commemorative materials, we found a nuanced depiction of grief in the story featuring a man experiencing loss, Oleksander, going against the gendered trope. A gendered depiction of soldiers was also nuanced in the materials by the depiction of a female sniper (SD) and a young female border guard (VG).

Visual tropes and memory

Comparing visualizations from three points in time, the first week, Bucha/Borodyanka, and the one-year mark, the most recurring visual figures we found in the material were women as victims and the male soldier. Another salient figure was the refugee which nevertheless ran counter to an othering, binary visualization of refugees as either victim or threat.

Symbolically, women typically represent "society", and the abuse of society is visualized through injured women, women crying in despair, and women performing community services such as carrying bread for relatives or neighbors. However, at the one-year mark, there were also pictures of female nurses, psychologists, and medics on or near the front. This would be a reflection of how Ukraine structured its armed forces and where they allowed women to serve and also how medical professionals participated in the civil defense and medical services as the war continued. Women and children expressing grief were still in visual focus in our material, more so than men, for example, in reportages about military funerals.

Male soldiers, another trope, were shown at the various stages of the conflict. Soldiers and life at or near the front were portrayed in several reportages, in our sample most visibly so near the one-year mark. This includes a TV reportage from an ambulance bus evacuating wounded soldiers (*SVT*), and a reportage series focusing on PTSD and treatment of physical and emotional injuries and rehabilitation of soldiers (*Expressen*). This and other stories foregrounded the vulnerability of soldiers who, in Ukraine, are primarily civilians taking up arms. This was a recurring theme throughout the year, shown in stories about men saying goodbye to their loved ones at the railway station (*VG*) or a peace activist fighting his inner demons after the war turned him into a fighter (*Aftenposten*). Thus, the role of men is twofold. As soldiers they represent the nation fighting for its independence, but as bereaved fathers and husbands they, like the grieving women, represent a war-impacted society.

Refugees, a salient trope in coverage of crises given the humanitarian concern with people fleeing, were prominent in our material from the beginning of the invasion, but less so at the one-year mark. The concrete explanation is that there may have been more people leaving Ukraine at the beginning and that, therefore, the story had high news value at that time. The invasion led to a mass exodus from Ukraine, and the humanitarian concern was urgent. Furthermore, this was the time when refugees were crossing the borders and the reception of Ukrainians was a topic in international as well as domestic Scandinavian news coverage. As noted above, we found that refugees were shown with agency, as active people responding to a difficult situation, not passive victims of the war. Sometimes civilian suffering was visualized by stories about domestic animals left behind because their owners had died or fled. In these cases, the cats and dogs represented a relatable normalcy disrupted by the war.

The visual figures that photojournalism draws upon are part of its language and genre and recognizable to the public, in this case as war photography. It is a balancing act for image-makers and editors selecting images, to use the familiar language while avoiding "foregrounding iconographic conventions rather than journalistic criteria of impact or accuracy" (Zarzycka & Kleppe 2013, p. 991). This challenge and drive, to find a fresh and authentic way to tell a story, was discussed by photojournalists in our interviews (see Chapter 3). Our analysis showed a prevalence of familiar but more nuanced tropes than those found in former studies of e.g. photo contests (Zarzycka & Kleppe

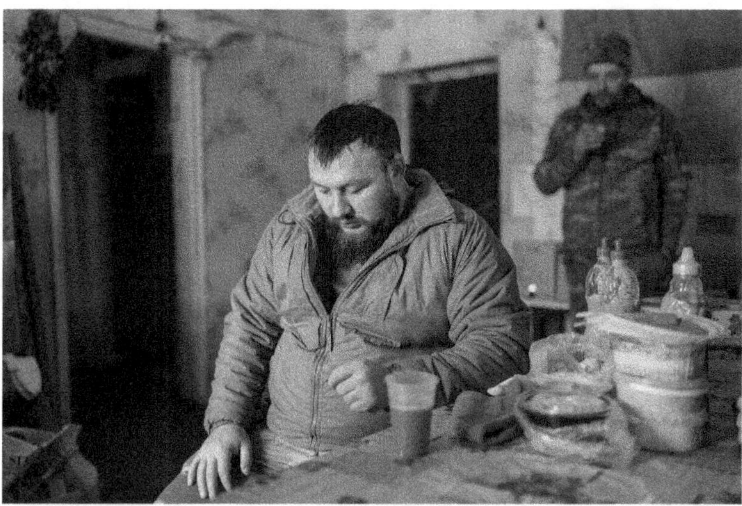

Figure 2.4 Years of fighting takes its toll on the Ukrainian soldiers. Photograph from the two-year mark. Photo by Aage Aune, TV 2. Reproduced with permission.

2013) and front-page photographs (Chouliaraki & Stolic 2017). The contrast could no doubt be context since we are looking at the images in their published context. Another reason could be that, as Zarzycka and Kleppe found in their study of World Press Photo entries, tropes do not appear in all images and are most commonly found in the single image where the metaphoric language is most condensed. In contrast, visual stories, such as the reportage, may offer opportunities for a sustained encounter and space for visibility as well as a more complex visual language (Newton 2001). Yet another reason could be that the Ukrainians, in the coverage, are portrayed as "people like us".

Chapter summary: witnessing through bridges and flows

This chapter has explored how image flows have affected the visual coverage of Ukraine during the first year of the Russian invasion and how witnessing through journalism may bridge the gap between the realities on the ground and the home audience in different ways. By exploring the networks through which the imagery travels, in "series, repetitions, sequences, rapid volleys", to quote Rubinstein and Sluis (2013, p. 154), we found some significant distinctions between the coverage from the visually (and politically) chaotic first week and the concentrated coverage of the atrocities in Bucha some weeks later.

During the first week, the imagery originated from a multitude of sources, such as government and military sources on both sides, influencers and social-media users, news agencies, in-house coverage by Scandinavian teams, and, of course, the many unknown sources of fake imagery. The witnessing aspects, as relayed in the published material, differed in the paper and online editions produced by the same outlets as well as between outlets. In the online editions, imagery tended to be integrated into the story, often offering mini-narratives in the form of image carousels or footage that supplemented the main story. On paper, we found more contrast between tabloids and subscription media than online. The subscription outlets tended to be more muted and also more selective in their visual choices, while the tabloids conveyed their visual messages through an active use of contrast and drama. The image sources, however, seem to be the most salient denominator when it comes to aspects of witnessing, along the axis between proximity and distance. In-house reporting from the field represents the strongest bridging between the war scenes and the audience as people in such stories are named and contextualized. Agency material, though strong with regard to visual quality, were mostly used as illustrations, in particular in news reporting from the home desk. As in-house reporting was scarce the first week, due to difficult working conditions, several news outlets tried to create an illusion of proximity by proxy using social-media entries published by Ukrainian civilians. They were sometimes illustrative but on several occasions used as the foundation for news stories in their own right.

The image flow from the atrocities in Bucha was of a different character as it was completely dominated by professional photojournalists. Agency and in-house photographers got access to the same motifs within the timespan of a few days, and here, the visual contribution of the in-house teams anchoring the atrocities to specific people and experiences was even more pronounced. Bucha also calls to attention the role of visibility in war reporting (Chouliaraki & Stolic 2017; Frosh 2011; Somerstein, 2020). Simultaneous atrocities in cities like Irpin and Borodyanka did not receive the same media attention as Bucha simply because they couldn't be visualized in the same thorough manner. As a result, the images from Bucha have taken on metonymic qualities as a symbol of Russian brutality in Ukraine as a whole.

In the third part of the chapter, we investigate the mnemonic qualities of news photography by looking at articulations of tropes and figures in published stories at the one-year mark. Tropes and figures point in two directions, both backward and forward. They build on former visual renderings, but they are more than just stereotypical quotations. As shown in the commemoration stories from 24 February 2023, we find that well-known themes from classic war reporting, such as the brave soldier and the suffering woman, are conveyed in nuanced and interesting ways. The commemoration stories are condensed summaries of the first year after the invasion, and as such they point towards the future as highlighting visualizations believed to be memorable.

According to Zelizer, war images tend to "gravitate toward the memorable" (2004, p. 116). Her point is that nested within the war images we find remnants of earlier wars as well as established understandings about "how war is supposed to be waged—notions about patriotism, sacrifice, humanity, the nation-state, and fairness that come as much from outside journalism as from within" (2004, p.115). Zelizer and other scholars studying visual war reporting (Chouliaraki 2017; Hariman & Lucaites 2007; Linfield 2010) have paid special attention to the single image, yet these are rare and not particularly salient to the material in our sample. This finding corroborates recent theory (Hariman & Lucaites 2018; Merrill 2023) about how digital virality affects iconicity processes in the media today. The images are numerous and, though often strong in content as well as visual quality, their individual impact is short-lived. The visual themes, however, rendered through a multitude of lenses seem to be more constant.

Notes

1 The number of news stories varies slightly from outlet to outlet, but the pattern is the same for all. All outlets except one in our sample produced more news stories the first week than the second week. The numbers do not include short news feed entries, only journalistically processed articles. Sometimes teams in the field worked together with teams at the home desk, and sometimes field assignments were assigned freelancers. As long as the stories were produced exclusively for the outlet in question, we have counted them as in-house reporting. Also see Chapter 1.
2 https://www.cbc.ca/news/world/ukraine-borodyanka-missing-civilians-1.6766732

3 The war next door

The perspectives of editors and photojournalists

The presence of Scandinavian journalists in Ukraine was unusually strong in the outlets' modern war reporting. This and can be linked to a widely adopted sentiment of geopolitical urgency in Norway and Sweden alike. Europe has not experienced territorial war since the dissolvement of Yugoslavia in the 1990s and the subsequent civil war between what is today Serbia, Croatia, and Bosnia. For Norway and Sweden (see Chapter 1), the war in Ukraine is fought close to their doorstep, which makes its destabilizing potential in the region a serious matter. A foreign editor in a Norwegian tabloid reports the outlet's highest readership ever in February 2022 and attributes this to a general fear of a new war in Europe. In the words of this editor, the first images were perceived as a visual reminder of the Second World War, and the shock effect was enhanced because "the [Ukrainians] look like us, their streets look like European cities, their wedding ceremonies look like ours, they are very recognizable".

In the previous chapter, we examined visual flows at the beginning of the invasion, looked at how visuals conveyed visibility in the coverage of atrocities, and identified visual icons and tropes in the commemorative stories at the one-year mark. We continue our exploration of journalistic witnessing and boundaries in this chapter, through interviews with editors and photojournalists. Specifically, this chapter addresses how routines and professional roles shape the visual coverage from Ukraine, with a specific focus on the work delivered by the news outlets' in-house teams. Although agency material is numerically the most important, in-house coverage was more highly valued by respondents.

Witnessing through journalism, discussed in the previous chapter through visual and bi-modal analyses, is a mediated process that begins with the physical encounter between the image-maker and the person or event photographed. We address this in the interviews by focusing on how routines and the individual experience shape witnessing in the photographic moment. This includes how photojournalists perceive themselves as eyewitnesses, touching on what one respondent referred to as "the gap between seeing and showing".

DOI: 10.4324/9781003478072-3

Our analytical tool is the concept of gatekeeping, referring to editorial selection processes and factors shaping them at various levels, according to the model developed by Shoemaker and Vos encompassing five levels: individual factors, routines, the organization, and, externally, social institutions and social systems (Shoemaker & Vos 2009; Vos 2020). For our purpose, individual factors and routines are the most relevant. In our sample, there is no common organizational structure, making it hard to compare editorial structures between outlets in a meaningful way. This is partly because several outlets have re-organized over the last couple of years and partly because they have responded differently to the economic and technological challenges facing the media industry over the past few decades. Boundaries between journalists, photojournalists, multiskilled reporters, still-photo, and television photographers are also progressively blurred, making professional roles more fluid. Our sample includes photojournalists who produce text, journalists who produce visuals, television professionals who produce stills, and editors who sometimes report from the field. Newsroom routines, however—which may include production routines, news value, resources, perceptions of audiences, competition and professional roles (Vos 2020), are still relevant to the gatekeeping aspects of our study.

Editors determine what constitutes quality, newsworthy, and ethical coverage while simultaneously negotiating the influx of materials from multiple outside sources. Photojournalists and multiskilled reporters also perform a gatekeeping routine by deciding what and how to photograph and which images to file, and their work on location includes negotiating with various external factors, for example, gaining access to relevant sites. The gatekeeping concept thus helps us address how, to speak with Vos (2020), the *function* of gatekeeping works as part of a news value-based routine and how the *role* of gatekeeping is articulated in a particular situation. Vos draws a useful distinction between the two, in order to emphasize that in the *role*, "certain actors in the information environment see it as their duty or responsibility to pass along some information and not other forms or kinds of information" (Vos 2016, cited in Vos 2020, p. 93).

Our editor respondents, 28 in total, represent all but one of the outlets included in our study. They include editors assigning photographers and responsibility for some aspect of the on-location coverage from Ukraine, editors selecting visuals for publication, and editors on the management level, with their respective practices determining topics discussed in interviews. The parts of the interviews discussed in this chapter focused on routines for visualizing the conflict and in-house coverage on location, how audience/user relations are understood, challenges with how to show the human cost of war, and perceived challenges with the strong pro-Ukrainian bias in the coverage. Routines concerning image verification discussed by editors will be presented in Chapter 4, which deals with verification and source criticism at the home desk.

We interviewed eight photojournalists working in either of the two countries, including five staff photojournalists or multiskilled reporters and three freelancers contributing to outlets in our study as well as other outlets in Scandinavia and other regions. Their age span is from 26 to 60, yet most have broad experience covering conflict, and a majority have covered Ukraine extensively, including prior to and during the full-scale Russian invasion. Our interviews touched on their experience working in Ukraine and other conflicts, routines for working on location in Ukraine, how to show the conflict, and the role of photojournalists. Both genders are represented in the sample. However, gender is not a defining marker in this study and is only discussed here in relation to specific experiences. Verification and credibility, addressed by photojournalists as part of their responsibility when on assignment, will be discussed in this chapter.

The findings are presented according to three salient topics emerging in the interviews: being on location and keeping the public at home engaged; witnessing and showing the human cost of war; and handling access and bias. We found few differences between the countries but rather contrasts between different types of outlets, from breaking news-focused tabloids on one end to public-service outlets on the other.

Being there

For most news outlets in our sample, the coverage of Ukraine has been part of an ongoing focus on the region dating back to the Maidan uprising that began in late 2013 and the Russian annexation of the Crimean Peninsula in 2014. Traditionally, the region has been covered with a strong focus on Russia, and the larger outlets had residential correspondents stationed there at the outbreak of the invasion (at the time of writing, two still have presence in Russia). Yet, to one of our respondents, a person under the age of 30, Ukraine belonged to the category "forgotten conflicts" until the rumors of an imminent Russian invasion started to spread in the beginning of 2022.

Several newsrooms had teams in Ukraine in the days prior to the full-scale invasion, as tensions in the region were escalating, and some had teams there on 24 February reporting live. Once the breaking news phase abated, the strategy for coverage shifted to the course of the war and its impact. With one exception, all newsrooms opted for a strong in-house presence in Ukraine in the early phase of the invasion, sending reporter-photographer teams there several times, some with rotating teams on a two-to-three week basis or more sporadic trips, and some with correspondents on location in Ukraine. In the words of one editor, "It was important to see for ourselves". Another stressed the advantages of having their own, exclusive material from "one of the most important events since World War II".

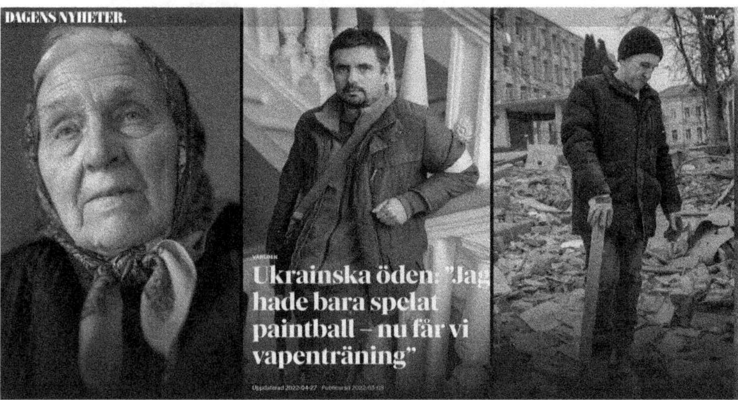

Figure 3.1 "Ukrainian destinies", reported and photographed by the newspaper team during the first two weeks of the invasion. Photos by Paul Hansen and Anders Hansson, *Dagens Nyheter*. Screenshot. Reproduced with permission.

As discussed in Chapter 2, the in-house visual coverage of the war was percentage-wise a small part of the overall news coverage, which visually drew mostly from international agencies. Furthermore, strategies for on-location presence differed, depending on journalistic focus and resources. According to an editor in the outlet that covered the war mostly from home, the reason for not going was lack of trained personnel: "We haven't prioritized foreign news for a long time. And you can't send someone who doesn't want to go to a war zone. It's not safe".

Others eventually reduced their presence because they prioritized breaking news from the home desk, while some continued their on-location reporting trips, though traveling less during 2023. Several respondents attributed this partly to the Ukrainian war developing into trench warfare, thus providing less visually interesting stories, and partly to the international focus prioritizing the Middle East after the Hamas attack on Israel on 7 October 2023. As explained by one editor in a Norwegian tabloid:

> We covered Ukraine in-depth all through the summer of 2023, but with 7 October and Gaza, we just put it aside. We are not a public-service institution, so we don't have the luxury of having people assigned to Sudan, Latin America and China. We go all in on one conflict at the time, because… if we are to compete with the bigger media, we have to prioritize. Still, when the dust settled after the first shocking events in Israel and Palestine, people started to tell us that we shouldn't forget that there was still another war going on. And in 2024, we started traveling to Ukraine again.

The public-service news outlets in both countries have provided the most regular in-house news coverage reporting from Ukraine, explained by respondents as part of their charter "to inform the public". However, a few subscription-based outlets also prioritized long-term presence. According to one such correspondent, the advantage of staying in the country full time is the ability to understand the undertows in society and get a feel for the changing phases: "Even if things look normal to outsiders, it doesn't mean that it actually is normal. People went on with their daily lives, but they were heavily traumatized and most people knew somebody at the front".

Staying full time permitted this correspondent to get to know more people and to establish trust: "I believe [living in the country] makes people more willing to open up". It also made it possible to work on more in-depth stories in periods with less action.

Most respondents were interviewed a year or more into the full-scale invasion. Some referred to the different phases of the conflict to explain their strategies, including this visual editor:

> There are different approaches to coverage in each phase: The beginning, when everything was uncertain, then the continued war and the direct impact, and then the long-term effects, for example: What is the effect on children, on families, on health care, on society, as the war continues? So, we did different types of stories in the different phases, for example a reportage about a large number of premature babies being born, a phenomenon found a year in, and likely an effect of the war.

Remote agencies, present staff

Visuals produced by staff photographers or contracted freelancers were preferred by most editors for in-depth stories, referred to as "the explanatory news experience" by one editor. While agency imagery was widely used when covering breaking news, it was also perceived by several editors as somewhat "remote". In-house teams allowed for a more personalized approach and were considered the most trustworthy. According to this visual area chief, being in the field provided an opportunity to "maybe get a bit closer and show more, knowing the circumstances and that the images were made ethically. We don't have that context with agency imagery". The importance of being able to provide context was echoed in the words of one multiskilled reporter, who was otherwise appreciative of the high-quality work delivered by the agencies and particularly their extensive use of Ukrainian photographers. For this reporter, a lack of context limits a journalistic image in a problematic way as it becomes reduced to a mere illustration:

> You know, when we settle for illustrations, we settle for something that could have been better. We waive our responsibility as journalists and

> communicate that these areas are not important enough for us to visit. Also, we let others take the risks we should be taking ourselves.

To satisfy the audience

Several editors said that their readers appreciated their in-depth, unique coverage and that reader preferences were a consideration in their coverage. For instance, two Swedish outlets assigned teams of well-known authors and senior photojournalists to produce reportages and series from Ukraine at various points, reminiscent of the classical reportage book and war reportage and published in culture or weekend sections. These initiatives, in line with the subscription-based outlets' profiles in general, were described as "hugely popular". We did not find this approach among the Norwegian outlets, although they also published popular reportages and in-depth stories. The reportages can be seen as an assertion of photojournalistic quality, both within the news organization and outward as a competitive edge.

One outlet that meticulously registers clicks and audience reading time was particularly set on keeping women and young readers satisfied. Teams in the field in Ukraine could be instructed to focus more on "soft stories" than military strategy if the numbers showed a declining interest among female readers. An editor in this outlet believed that, although the idea of securing women readership is good, the strategy is sometimes misguided:

> I don't believe women get hooked just because they see images of other women. I believe the interesting distinction is between tactics on the frontline and the consequences of war. And in my book, the consequences of war are always the most important, regardless of gender and age.

The assertion of a unique in-house approach was articulated by another editor explaining the aim of reaching readers, an indirect reference to the visual image flows we discussed in Chapter 2:

> I feel there's a wish and almost a hunger for the type of stories that add something extra, that take risks in portraying an event and that also has a unique visual language, a unique, not interpretation, but its own type of story in the midst of the flow of stories. This doesn't mean that you exclude other stories, but it means that you choose and curate and show another aspect.

Several newsrooms in our study have experienced cutbacks among photojournalism staff in recent years. While some compensate with a stronger focus on live TV, the resources placed on Ukraine were described as a boost to the documenting and storytelling practices within the visual area. In the words of one experienced photojournalist: "Photojournalism has received an increase

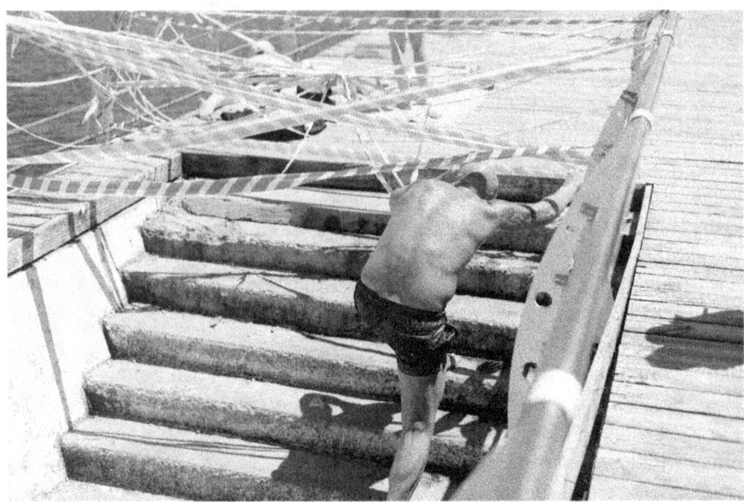

Figure 3.2 A swimmer defies the government's advice to not swim in the mined water outside Odesa. Photo by Kyrre Lien, *VG*. Reproduced with permission.

in focus and importance [in the news outlet]. That doesn't bring us any more resources, but at least management is applauding what we achieve".

Finding the unique angle

Editors as well as photojournalists considered maintaining reader's interest a challenge as other world events sidelined Ukraine in the public consciousness, especially the Hamas attack on Israel on 7 October 2023 and the ensuing war in Gaza. However, our overview of the coverage (see Chapter 1) showed that the news outlets did not publish fewer stories about Ukraine after the outbreak of war in Gaza. Comments on this point also referred to finding unique angles, which respondents said was difficult in a conflict fought in the trenches where visual perspectives and access are limited, a comment echoing the photojournalists, including this respondent:

> The problem is when it's no longer a news focus. But there's still war in Ukraine. That's a challenge for us. It's not news that people are dying every day, which is terrible. Then you'll do a reportage about the fact that it's no longer news, and then what? Then you do a cultural (feature) reportage. So now, two years in, what do we do? Yet another crying woman in

> front of a destroyed building. And you have to do that, but it becomes almost repetitive for us and for the readers.

Another photojournalist reflected on a challenge related to online publishing which, to this respondent, is more demanding than "old-fashioned" newspaper production:

> Before, we could settle for 4–5 good pictures, but now you need a lot more. In a story of some 10 000 characters, you need maybe 12 pictures to break up the text. We register that people can't bear to deal with long stretches of text, and this means that a great many reports require the photographers to work even more thoroughly with the cases.

The staff photojournalists interviewed have all traveled to Ukraine on several assignments in the past two years, while the freelancers' experience includes assignments and working independently on projects without deadlines. Some said there has been a certain flexibility in covering stories, such as if the team discovers a story while on assignment, they could explore them along the way. Photojournalists with previous knowledge of the area reported that they were usually free to pursue their own ideas. One said the stories produced were based on "a combination of my ideas and intentions and a gut feeling about what might interest others". Another photojournalist stressed the importance of being selective when pitching ideas to editors:

> I always have about 40 ideas in my head, but I don't throw them all in the air when I pitch them. At that moment, I'm always very clear on how I want an idea to look, if it's news or features, how I want to proceed, what camera I will use. This makes it easier for the people at home to imagine what the story will look like. And since I have a visual mind, I'm usually able to describe my projects in words. I don't think I ever got a no.

Although some photojournalists noted that they were not the ones making the ultimate decision about stories since those are determined by the news flow and editors at the home desk. Freelancers said they appreciated the flexibility to be able to stop and cover the entirety of an event and its aftermath, like attending a funeral the day after an attack killing civilians, while news photographers on deadline had to leave the day before. One respondent, a documentary photographer who also takes assignments for the news media, appreciated "not having to explain myself to an editor on a daily basis".

From the perspective of photojournalists, the search for fresh angles was also described as a creative drive. In the words of one respondent:

> The visual quotes, the details that hit you emotionally, that's what I'm looking for, although it's really difficult... The bodies in the body bags are everywhere, and that's hard... But the small things that can become universal, those are really powerful.

Strategies mentioned by other respondents include trying to display beauty in unexpected surroundings, for instance, a retreat center for soldiers suffering from war trauma, or, more commonly, to render the daily lives of Ukrainians understandable for Scandinavians by visiting beaches, hairdressers working without electricity, or revisiting dramatic sites to see people rebuild their lives. In the words of one photojournalist: "to find the small narratives that speak about something much bigger". Another respondent emphasized that life, even at war, is more than trenches and suffering: "People try to get on with their lives. And it's not the case that all Ukrainians are deadly serious all the time, even if it looks that way in the media".

Photojournalistic witnessing

Several respondents described their commitment to covering Ukraine as a story they had pursued in some cases for several years. One photojournalist spoke of the war as "the most important conflict of our time", articulating the role of the photojournalist as witness (Griffin 2010; Linfield 2010). Being a witness was described by this photojournalist as relevant on several levels, for the people who experience war and also on behalf of the audience at home:

> The word witness... it sounds like you have to be present at the scene when something horrible, like a massacre, is committed. But witnessing is also when you meet individuals and tell their stories. Because war is about abuse. So, I'm a witness on behalf of my readers, that's how I see it. And also, because the threshold for committing atrocities may get higher. Not that the Russians will stop bombing because we're there, but maybe some smaller things will not happen with reporters present.

All photojournalists said they believed their work had a purpose and several respondents said they appreciated being able to work on longer stories and follow-up pieces reconnecting with people encountered previously. This requires time and resources not always available in international coverage but which some of the outlets allocated to Ukraine during the first year. Describing the role of the photojournalist as a "catalyst", one respondent said part of the job was not primarily photographing but rather facilitating connections on the scene. Another pointed out the sometimes blurred boundaries between staff photographers and reporters in a field team: "Who takes the picture is not so important. What is important is to agree on how we can get access, how we can do better, how to be safe". Image-makers saw their work as a complement to that of international agency photographers and to Ukrainian photojournalists as their roles were positioned in different ways. In the words of this respondent:

> The Ukrainians live their story. This is their lives, their neighbors and their country that they are covering. They have a completely different presence and tell the story in a different way. They are so close. But being that close you might not see everything. Because they see the little things that we might not see. We see the exclamation marks and they see that someone's garden has been destroyed, maybe it meant a lot to grandma. They have a completely different tonality.

Another photojournalist agreed but from a somewhat different perspective:

> My mother argued that there are so many great photographers in Ukraine, so why should I risk my life to go there? She has a point. Ukrainian photographers are great, and I don't know if the world needs my pictures. But what is really important to me is that we need as many stories and images as possible as a way to fight propaganda and unilinear perspectives.

Cultural differences, such as differences in professional decorum, were also echoed in an episode from a Ukrainian funeral in 2022, related by one respondent: "The Ukrainian photographers wondered why we chose to stay in the back. They have a different tradition, but we try to avoid photographing people in shock, so we chose to wait for a day".

Photographing frontlines

Competition between news outlets and within the newsroom was another factor mentioned as shaping routines since the space afforded a story depended on the news flow and also on the quality or "edge" of the work. As the war moved into the trenches, an editor complained that frontline images often became too generic to spark an interest:

> It doesn't really matter if it is us or the New York Times who visits the frontline. You have the soldier protecting his ears before firing artillery, the soldier smoking in the trenches or jumping into the trenches to convey some action. It is really, really similar and it could be from anywhere.

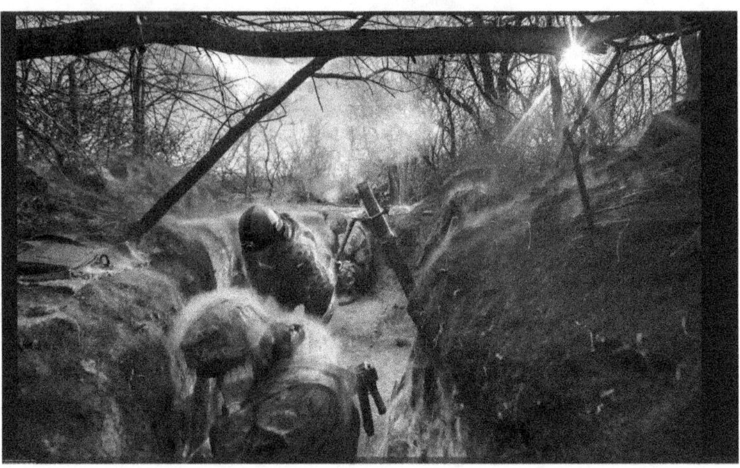

Figure 3.3 Ukrainian soldiers firing from their position near Bachmut, Donetsk. Part one of a three-part reportage series from the front. Photo by Paul Hansen, *Dagens Nyheter*. Screenshot. Reproduced with permission.

One photojournalist spoke of the drama and emotion attributed to photographs of conflict:

> In the beginning, you could photograph a burned-out tank and it was, "wow". But now, you have to get closer and are almost expected to end up close to the fighting yourself [for the images to garner attention].

Other photojournalists recognized the phenomenon but ascribed it to the combination of outside demands and the war photographer's own need for action:

> For the photographers, the sadness of everyday life at war can also be generic. And 80 percent of the Ukrainians lead quite normal lives... But conflict photographers are often drawn to adrenalin. They want to be in the trenches, they want images of mitral valves and bomb launchers. It's kind of a macho thing, but it doesn't only relate to men. It's also a photographer thing. It's visual, it's drama... I don't know if you should write this, but some photographers have like a list... I need a funeral – check, someone grieving – check, a dead person, an explosion...

Most agreed that you need both civilian life and frontline drama to be able to show war. One photographer noted that, while civilians were harder to photograph in a visually interesting way, the trenches were visual but provided little information: "The soldiers rarely say anything interesting. It's mostly dangerous to be there, in a way".

Photojournalists also brought up the danger of gamification of the war visuals, which they found to be partly related to generic frontline pictures that one claimed "turns soldiers into robots in uniform" and partly to the use of satellites and drones published online by the brigades. "Drone videos can be very important material, but they are often remote and highly dehumanizing. It's like watching a video game on a cloudy screen, and it can make you forget that people are actually getting killed", one photojournalist said. An editor explained that it was not necessarily the material as such that was the problem, but the way it was publicized:

> Titles like "Look how the Russians are running. They didn't know what would hit them", using footage from social media or dramatic scenes shared by the Ukrainian army on Twitter [contribute to gamification]. There are three groups of such visuals in journalism; the social-media images shared by the army to score propaganda points, images from massacres and civilian suffering and front-line imagery. But I think they matter less today.

The gap between seeing and showing

Photojournalists often have to make decisions about how to photograph people in vulnerable situations. While the appropriate photographic distance was described by respondents as contingent on the circumstances, there was agreement that the photojournalist had an ethical responsibility to portray people respectfully, for instance, by stepping back or framing them in a way that does not expose injuries or the face of a victim. They also concurred that it was the photographer's responsibility to document the scene and the editor's task to make the appropriate selection for the story. Although some, like this photographer, said they sometimes refrained from sending certain photos:

> I always try to show reality. On the front, straight up and as close as possible, sometimes perhaps too close. Though if it's too close, and it's just a picture of flesh, then it has the opposite effect.

The challenge of photographically conveying events on the ground to a distant public is a major theme in the literature on witnessing (see Chapters 1 and 2). One of the photographers interviewed referred to this experience as a "gap" between seeing and showing:

> The Ukrainians want us to show the essence of it as straightforwardly as possible. They want to communicate what is happening in their country. And if you step outside of Ukraine, you may see the opposite…You can

> tell the story, but in the moral we live here. In a way, of course, you need to stay in touch with the viewer and the reader. You don't need to scare them off, but sometimes you might wake them up because reality in Ukraine is more brutal than what we show here.

For editor respondents, the revelation of the massacre in Bucha in early April 2022 appeared to have been a turning point when it comes to visualizing the human toll of the conflict, as it resulted in the publication of visuals showing dead civilians laying in the streets and buried in mass graves left behind by the occupying Russian forces (see Chapter 2 for analyses of visuals from this event). In the words of this respondent: "We are usually extremely restrictive, but it was our moral duty to show what it looked like in the streets".

However, compared to previous conflicts, the deliberations over explicit imagery did not appear to be as challenging in the coverage of Ukraine, even as the news outlets published more images of casualties than they would normally do. According to this editor, "as long as it is within the boundaries of what is ethical, I believe we have a duty to show the hard sides of reality. It may be rough, but it shouldn't be vulgar or splatter, [the image] has to protect people's dignity". Another referred to not printing explicit material as "the easiest way out" and a form of dishonesty; "For people to understand how horrible it is we have to show them something".

One photojournalist in our sample was critical of this approach, arguing that graphic violence is never dignified: "I oppose showing too much violence. I don't think it makes the people in the images relatable. I think they get dehumanized". One of the broadcast outlets struggled with the same dilemmas but added that it is not always a question of an image being graphic or not, according to this editor: "It depends on the way you tell the story. You shouldn't lead with the strongest images, but rather integrate them into the story".

These comments speak to the various factors found to shape gatekeeping for visuals: ethical and moral deliberations concerning victims (Mortensen et al. 2017) and concerns with audience reactions (Allan 2014) and with public opinion (Zelizer 2005). Although criticism of the massive focus on Ukraine reached some interviewed editors, nobody said they received complaints about showing victims of the war in Ukraine.

Editors said they were not swayed or pressured by visuals available outside journalism, thus asserting their gatekeeping position. However, there was a contrast between subscription-based outlets that rarely used visual content mined from social media and former afternoon paper outlets, where editors said they routinely mined social media for story ideas, curating the content.

The visibility of modern conflict and crisis on social media has brought the debate about what to show into the open, forcing a kind of transparency on journalism (Mortensen et al. 2017).[1] We found this in our analysis of the coverage of Bucha (see Chapter 2) where, in some articles, editors shared their decisions to publish certain images. According to this visual editor, staffers following events closely may be more inclined to publish certain pictures:

> I think photo desks in general are more for having the courage to publish. You get a little held back by the managing editor who has the ultimate responsibility. They are further away from the publication process, and they don't follow the visual image feed. So sometimes you might go for an easier solution than you would have needed to.

Experience from covering previous wars helped some respondents go through the visual image feeds from Ukraine, including this editor addressing the explicitness of visuals and the propaganda component of materials reaching newsrooms today:

> I don't think this conflict stands out. At the same time, I think that we, the media, – or at least I hope that we – learn and get better at processing images compared to say during ISIS [Syria]and that period. It was so new for us to be used as propaganda by a foreign power that maybe you didn't take that into consideration when you needed the website views. And now I think you are more transparent, saying: "we know that this is propaganda, but we think it is important to publish this because…" But maybe that's just my wishful thinking, and maybe I've just gotten better at it – hopefully – as a publicist.

Several editors said that the war in Ukraine has sparked more newsroom discussions about routines and the ethics of visualizing conflict, something they found positive.

The appropriate place and time to show conflict imagery was also addressed by photojournalists. While some believed certain images could not be published in a Scandinavian news outlet, some said it might become a historical record or be published in another context later on, such as in a book (Figure 3.4).[2]

Safety, bias, and trust

Issues related to safety shaped the work of the teams on assignment in Ukraine, apparently a bigger concern for editors than for the photojournalists interviewed. "I've had some sleepless nights, considering the safety risks involved in sending people into a war zone", one editor said. "Yet, to understand how Ukrainians live, we need to be there". In both countries, the focus on safety and first aid has been steadily growing in recent years. In Norway, it was partly triggered by a Norwegian reporter being shot and killed by a Taliban group at the Serena hotel in Afghanistan in 2008.[3] The Swedish news media are also aware of the risks, as a Swedish public-broadcast Sveriges

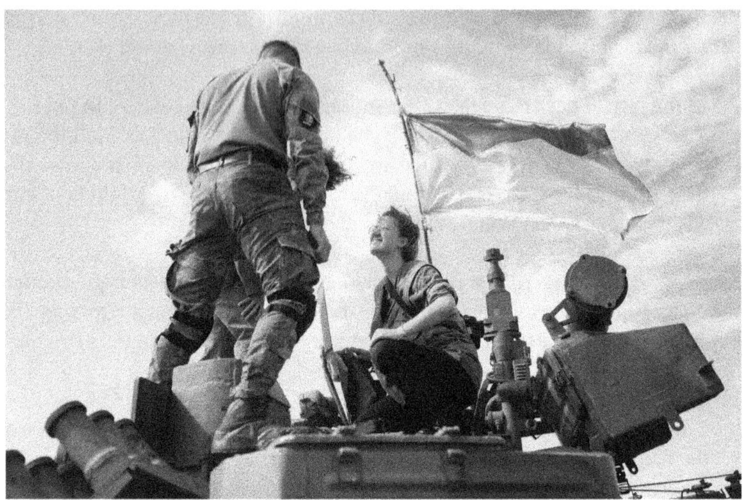

Figure 3.4 A multiskilled reporter interviewing soldiers on top of a Ukrainian tank. Photo by Jan T. Espedal, *Aftenposten*. Reproduced with permission.

Radio Asia correspondent was shot and killed in Kabul, Afghanistan, in 2014,[4] and Swedish journalists have been kidnapped in war zones.[5] Editors described a learning process where experience on location and in-house support systems in place improved chances of reporting from high-risk areas. This included always traveling in teams, mandatory daily debriefings, rotations, and required time off for returning correspondents. Some commented on a lack of in-house experience and preparedness for on-location coverage after years of reduced international travel, leading to a steeper learning curve and a coverage that was further away from the front and "a few steps behind the war photographers".

The editors interviewed stressed that they only sent staff who volunteered to go to Ukraine and obliged them to go through safety training. The majority of the interviewed photojournalists were experienced war reporters, most with previous knowledge of Ukraine, but some were fresh in the field. None of them claimed to be easily scared, but all had experienced getting too close to the action from time to time. One got a little jumpy after the Russian attack on a pizza joint in Kramatorsk where journalists and relief workers used to gather at night. This was not a hangout for soldiers, and the respondent considered it a direct attack on the international media. Another ended up too close to the frontline and had to take cover in a small ditch when the Russians started their bombardment: "That was terrible. You can't leave, because then you will get shot. It was a small hole in the ground and all we could hope for was that they weren't firing arms that would blow up the dirt". One claimed the most dangerous situation occurred at the beginning of the war, when armed Ukrainians patrolled the streets of Kyiv at night: "They were stressed and hadn't slept for days. We met them in an alley after curfew. That was dangerous".

The strengthened safety measures in some newsrooms included geotagging their teams, to be able to locate them at all times. One newsroom also hired a safety producer to go with the teams. As explained by its foreign editor: "The safety producer is someone who works with me on safety issues so that the team can concentrate on other parts of the logistics. It's quite common in international newsrooms".

The tracking devices were perceived by some photojournalists as inducing a false sense of safety. Some respondents avoided using them, partly for fear of being located by the wrong people if the tracking device was connected to satellites and partly because tracking would not provide immediate help in an emergency. In the words of one reporter: "if something happens, the real help would be the people you're with".

Access to danger

The ability to move around in Ukraine was described as changing throughout the course of the conflict, with a general openness to international journalists but with restrictions due to dangerous zones whose location shifted throughout the conflict. Although, as one respondent said, "everywhere is dangerous in Ukraine", a factor of a war with constant attacks. Another emphasized how risks may differ from place to place: "In Kyiv it is usually quite safe, but then you have a "missile Monday" where the missiles are pouring down. In Donbas the risk is always high, and in Lviv it is unpredictable".

Drones were considered a new danger when covering a story, as they have become an integral part of warfare in this conflict, and more dangerous than bombs. Said this photographer: "First they [the Russians] send a drone, and this is followed by another drone that films you as you die".

Access was also described as contingent on circumstances and changing depending on the events on the ground, a fluidity that also meant that sometimes agreed-upon access could turn into a no and vice versa:

> The quieter things are [on the front], the more difficult it is to get access. Each brigade has a press officer and when it's calm it's more difficult, and the more chaos and fighting the less they care about the journalists because they are focused on their soldiers.

Photojournalists sometimes wanted to get closer to the action than the editors allowed, and at other times they withdrew from assignments proposed by editors. One freelancer reported such negotiations as potentially uneasy situations:

> I have said no to a couple of assignments, because I had a bad feeling about them. Fortunately, the editors were cool, but you know, you don't want to be considered a coward or someone that cannot be trusted, so this always feels a little risky.

The same freelancer also commented on how different media outlets approached freelancers differently with regard to safety:

> Some expect you to carry the cost of safety equipment yourself, while others invest in you. One outlet bought me a new bulletproof west that cost them a ton of money. But some… when the war started, I was in [a dangerous zone] and one outlet called me to ask about the security situation because they were debating whether to send their own people there. No one asked me if I was safe. I got this absurd feeling that they assess the value of the body of a freelancer differently from the bodies of their own staff.

Getting access

Access to Ukraine was also mentioned by editors as well as photojournalists as better than in other regions where international journalists could not travel or were not given entry. Good access was mentioned as a key factor to why Ukraine was so prominent in the coverage during the first year of the invasion: "There is an infrastructure in place in Ukraine that works, and we have covered the region before and have experience and knowledge", one editor said, in part as a response to criticism they had received about their strong focus on Ukraine at the perceived expense of other regions. Respondents were in agreement that restrictions in Ukraine were relatively few and easy to understand. According to one broadcast respondent, such restrictions were mainly tactical and related to sites of military importance:

> We can lose our accreditation if we film… let's say an atomic plant, because it may reveal military positions. This is of course a limitation that we try to be open about. We try to get as close as possible, and in a stand-up we can explain what it is that we are not allowed to film and why.

Photojournalists are used to logistics planning, but in a foreign environment where they don't speak the language, they need assistance. Local "fixers" were described as trusted and skilled Ukrainians making the Scandinavian coverage possible. Fixers not only contribute to preparations and getting access to people and sites, their intimate knowledge of language and culture also provides safety for the journalist, if not always for themselves (Murrell 2015; Palmer 2019). According to this photojournalist, "their input and eyes are invaluable, as is their will and ability. So, we are very dependent on what the Ukrainians see".

Some fixers were provided by Ukrainian authorities, and one respondent referred to such relationships as "being embedded" and a fact of modern conflict reporting (e.g. Griffin 2010). One photojournalist referred to military fixers as part of "a macho culture" where the fixers behave "almost as soldiers". Working on stories about vulnerable civilians, this is not the best choice, according to this respondent. Other photojournalists worked with independent civilian fixers, often individuals who chose to help foreign reporters as a (relatively well paid) side job. Our respondents have worked with psychologists, IT consultants, theater directors, and advertising specialists, to mention a few. Usually, these fixers have been recruited through personal or semi-professional networks, and several do it for patriotic reasons. In successful collaborations, where the interpersonal chemistry is right, the relationships might turn into friendship.

The safety aspect of good relations with a fixer was expressed by one multiskilled reporter in these terms: "It helps to travel with someone you can trust, and that you can talk to afterwards. In sharp situations it is good to be able to speak honestly about security issues and about being frightened and all of that".

Gender balance in reporter/fixer teams can be of importance. Women may have easier access to other women but can also strike a protective chord among male soldiers. As one female photojournalist said, "they sometimes underestimate you a little, which can be an advantage because it seems to me that it helps them to unwind".

A good fixer understands what photojournalists need. They usually have broad personal networks and good social skills. One photojournalist spoke about intense periods in the field with a particularly committed fixer, with workdays lasting from 7 in the morning until midnight, every day for almost three weeks. However, some freelancers said they only rarely used fixers, as they mostly relied on other trusted sources for assistance, such as locals. This routine was explained as in part a budget factor as fixers can be quite expensive and also as a preference because it gave more flexibility.

However, safety is not only a physical matter (Muindi 2023). For the people in the field, the personal encounters with violence and suffering leave their marks. Several Ukrainian fixers experienced being retraumatized from trips to the frontlines. One multiskilled reporter was commissioned a crisis psychologist by the media outlet as a routine: "It was ok, but I prefer talking to people I trust in a more organic manner. It is just as helpful to talk to someone who has been in the same situation".

Two male photojournalists revealed that they decided to formalize their romantic relationship with their partners back home as a reaction to their experiences. As recounted by one of them:

> I have been doing this for a long time. I believe I am capable of handling it, and I don't suffer from PTSD or anything, but it makes an impression. And since I have started writing as well as photographing, I seem to get more emotionally invested. There are too many semi-alcoholics and people with broken relationships in this profession. And if you only see death and destruction, decade after decade, it does something to you. So, I have decided to hold on to life, in a way.

Access as bias

A lack of access to parts of Ukraine under Russian control and to Russia itself was mentioned as a gap in the coverage by editors as well as photojournalists. A one-sided coverage and bias favoring the Ukrainian perspective were also brought up in most interviews, echoing findings in research about a "patriotic journalism" in war coverage (Bergman & Hearns-Branaman 2024; Nygren & Widholm 2024). Reasons given for this imbalance included a widespread distrust of Russia, a lack of information from Russia-controlled areas of Ukraine, a strong identification with Ukraine, and a view of Russia as the aggressor. Editors as well as photojournalists said that they were aware of this bias and that there was propaganda on both sides. However, respondents also articulated a difference, in their view, between the one side offering information—Ukraine—and Russia, which did not offer verifiable information. According to this editor:

> It's not just that you do the bidding of someone and their interests. You can also see it as, they are making it possible for something to become public. I think it's difficult, because as soon as you're assisted by Ukrainian authorities it's propaganda. I don't think it's that simple. It depends a lot on the situation and the possibilities for us to travel in these areas.

Another editor described the coverage as "wildly unilateral" but explained it by referring to the lack of access to Russia and Russia-controlled areas: "We apply for visas all the time, but so far without avail. And on the other side, you have a friendly army who takes you all the way to the front". What gets lost is the nuances in the war, according to one photojournalist with experiences dating back to 2014:

> There are always two parties in a war, and you have to listen to both, even if you disagree. Or… at least you should try to understand how they rationalize what they do. We don't have access to Russia, but I think we

> could have focused more on people in Eastern Ukraine where people feel more connected to Russia, or at least the former Soviet Union. Not that they all approve of the invasion, but they see things differently from the people in Kyiv.

Another editor described the challenge of approaching people with standpoints that oppose the main narrative:

> Even if they say yes, we have to consider the risks they are running by talking to us. We have to anonymize them, so it is impossible to depict them as intimately as others. The main discourse is quite heavy… Then again, it's not that these views are not out in the open, but in the big picture I am not sure that it really counts… for the political side at home, that is.

One editor believed that time has made it easier to write more critical stories. As an example, this editor mentioned how young Ukrainian men were forced to join the army. "The way they recruit is quite rough. But this is also a fact of this war that has changed over the years".

There were several examples of stories published in the news outlets that addressed long-term effects and the personal cost to Ukrainians, such as the aforementioned stories about premature babies, a series on PTSD among Ukrainian soldiers, and a story on Russian prisoners of war in a Ukrainian prison. However, some respondents said there were more critical stories that could be covered, such as corruption in Ukraine and Ukrainian Trump supporters, both topics mentioned by respondents interviewed in 2024.

Photojournalists said that they had the freedom to work in Ukraine but that there were topics with limited access, including photographing fallen Ukrainian soldiers, except for military funerals that have been covered by several of our respondents. Said one photojournalist: "This is what it's like to cover conflict. When you're embedded you have to show that perspective, and if you're too critical you might not be able to come back". According to another image-maker:

> I would love to cover the other side, because on the other side you find the same victims, just from other cities, because it's the politics and the military deciding, and the people (fighting) on the front they don't have a say. Some of them don't even want to be there.

The desire to cover the regions of Russia was articulated by editors at the larger news outlets. This requires experience and language skills, either through in-house foreign correspondents or other Russian and Ukrainian-speaking staffers, which some, but not all, newsrooms invested in for their coverage. A lack of resources and preparedness for international coverage, including Russian and Ukrainian-speaking staff, were also found in previous research into this conflict (Nygren & Widholm 2022). (See Chapter 4 for a discussion about social media and verification).

Control of information

More broadly than the war in Ukraine, editors and photojournalists expressed concern about an increased control of information and the dangers facing correspondents who are often targeted in conflicts today. According to this editor, these circumstances may have a negative impact on journalistic quality and independence:

> In a way, the image flow becomes one-sided, because in war zones many countries' militaries work with embedded journalists. This is an old discussion, but it's not something that's going away. It's something that is embraced more and more, and becomes more and more controlled. So, it's harder and harder to work on your own. But we shouldn't romanticize the past and World War II when photographers went and got themselves blown up. Journalists in the past worked in a way that no employer today would sign off on. But it's difficult not to be controlled because it's so tightly regulated.

Generative AI was seen by editors as well as photojournalists as an emerging threat that may raise doubts in people's minds even about authentic images. Though not related only to the war in Ukraine, the technology has developed rapidly within the past year. One photojournalist described sometimes choosing to use an analog camera, in part because in certain situations it inspires more trust than a digital camera that can be used to transmit images quickly and in part for verification purposes since negatives are proof of origin.

Photojournalists mentioned trust as part of their own credibility as image-makers and also as something that is difficult to achieve in the digital news coverage:

> Our credibility comes from the fact that we are there, we can verify, we photograph and convey the story we see. Readers should be able to trust that… The reader should know that you're the one standing there taking the picture. So the image is true in that sense, but it should not be used in other contexts.

A widespread distrust makes the role of journalism to assert authenticity more important, according to several respondents, a topic to be explored in the next chapter. Photojournalists said the widespread doubt about images makes their responsibility greater. According to this image-maker:

> We have known for a long time that you can lie with pictures, but now you can create pictures out of nothing…We are extremely aware of the fact

> that our credibility is our greatest asset…In the past, I think you took the authenticity of the photograph for granted, but you don't do that anymore. And I think that's good, because you have to work to earn trust.

Visual trust was also described as a part of spending time with people. Photojournalists said that when they get time to get to know people and tell nuanced stories, they receive positive reactions from their audiences. According to one photojournalist, this doubles back to relatability in the accounts:

> It's hard to put your finger on what it is. I think it's mainly an emotion. When you see someone that you think you could like or love, the story becomes closer. But you need time to develop trust between the photographer and the people photographed.

Chapter summary: about the coverage of the war next door

The purpose of being on location in Ukraine for the Scandinavian news outlets was explained by respondents as covering an important story and as providing a more closeup and less generic perspective than news agencies (Caple 2019). A focus on unique in-house stories was considered as a way to keep the public at home engaged and as an assertion of quality. However, the strategy of relying on clicks to trace audience preferences and reading time was questioned by some respondents for the way it shaped the coverage. The photojournalists, who volunteered to go to Ukraine, described their role as complementary to international and local image-makers and as contributing to multiple perspectives as a way to counter propaganda. Finding a unique angle was seen by the photojournalists in different ways, which appears in part related to their assignment and brief, ranging from a challenge given the increased demand for more images in digital publishing to a creative drive in the coverage.

Questions of how to show war and victims of violence, though not a new challenge and responsibility for journalists, emerged as in one sense less controversial here than in other conflicts, although the topic generated extended newsroom discussions about visual ethics. Editors and photojournalists appeared to agree that, as stated by one respondent: It's not just what you show, but how you show it (Hanusch 2012). The cautiousness of management and concerns with audience reactions were among the factors considered in deliberations over photographs (Allan 2014). While image selection is highly contextual, it was nevertheless the opinion of image-makers that you should take the picture but not necessarily show it. Respondents also brought up the concern with explicit visuals feeding into propaganda, such as in previous coverage of Syria. The lack of controversy over visuals and the lack of criticism from the public may be attributed to a public consensus about this conflict, in contrast to other, more polarizing crises, like the war in Gaza.

Access was considered comparably easy in Ukraine, in large part due to the Ukrainian "fixers" who were considered invaluable. However, security was discussed as a factor shaping the coverage. Editors described a strengthened routine and protocol in place, and several respondents said that familiarity and confidence had grown over time, enabling them to improve their coverage. Among photojournalists, security and risk were in part related to the danger on the ground, with weaponized drones considered a new danger. The psychological and emotional impact of witnessing the war was brought up by several respondents, as a factor impacting the Ukrainians in particular and also as something image-makers themselves experienced. All agreed that the coverage was one-sided and that there was a pro-Ukraine bias, attributed to the lack of access and lack of trust in Russian sources and Russia-controlled areas as well a consensus about a "war of good against evil" (Nygren & Widholm 2024). However, respondents interviewed recently with a two-year perspective of the conflict said that there could have been more nuance in the coverage.

The rise of generative AI was a topic that engaged the photojournalists in particular, because of its perceived impact on public trust in their own work. Some respondents said that photojournalists need to do more to show and maintain credibility. One point made, which will be discussed in the next chapter, is that credibility doesn't just have to do with the veracity of the image; it also has to do with routines for source criticism (Steensen et al. 2022) and the personal and professional ethics of the photographer in the encounter (Linfield 2010). The interviewed photojournalists appeared to see themselves as witnesses to the public despite and perhaps also because of a viral image culture offering unfiltered ways to see war. More broadly than the war in Ukraine, respondents expressed concern with an increased control of information in conflicts and crises and the risk to reporters that have become targets in war.

Editors as well as photojournalists appeared to see themselves as gatekeepers to a certain extent, expressing concern with misinformation and the ethics of visual information. However, as our respondents also noted, the gatekeepers on the ground and on social media control information flows reaching the public, which poses challenges, to be explored in the following chapter, about the efforts to ascertain truthfulness and build credibility.

While the asserted role of journalism is to inform the public, it is negotiated against competition and maintaining audience interest, as articulated in our interviews. Respondents described the coverage of this conflict as a process where they have raised the level of skill and confidence for international reporting. However, while photojournalism has asserted itself in several newsrooms, some respondents noted a lack of resources and expressed uncertainty about a long-term commitment (Caple 2019; Ferrucci et al. 2020; Gynnild et al. 2017; Mortensen & Keshelashvili 2013).

Notes

1 The 2015 publication and social-media virality of a photograph of a young Syrian boy, drowned in the Mediterranean as his family sought to reach safety, caused debate about the propriety and impact of its publication (e.g. Mortensen et al. 2017), yet was also found to evoke empathy (e.g. Proitz 2018).

2 This perspective has also been found among editors and photojournalists covering terror, such as Utøya in Norway in 2011, when Norwegian editors were found to delay publication of certain images until a later time when a traumatized audience was deemed ready to see them (Simonsen 2015).

3 https://www.nj.no/nyheter/skuddene-pa-serena-ble-en-vekker-for-journalistsikkerheten/

4 https://sverigesradio.se/artikel/5805981

5 https://www.dn.se/kultur-noje/bokrecensioner/magnus-falkehed-och-niclas-hammarstrom-i-dag-ska-vi-inte-do-fangar-i-krigets-syrien/.

4 Truth, trust (and everything in between)

Was Dalton Kennedy an American neo-Nazi enlisted in the Ukrainian army? Did the "Ghost of Kyiv" down 40 Russian fighter planes? Did Russian paratroopers cheer as they invaded Ukraine? Fake news and fake images create legends, and real footage from wars fought elsewhere creates misconceptions of the actual warfare. Modern digital technology, propaganda, disinformation, and misinformation have become integral to warfare and increasingly harder to detect. Truth claims emerge from all kinds of sources, and their rapid diffusion onto social media, websites, and the news media has created what Chouliaraki and Al-Ghazzi call "an ecology of distrust" in news dissemination (Chouliaraki & Al-Ghazzi 2022). Social-media platforms are seen as suspicious spaces of disinformation, and AI is variably coined as part of the problem (e.g. deep fakes) and part of the solution (digital-forensics methodologies).

In this situation, fact-checking represents an important boundary value in journalism (see Chapter 1). It is more than a method and can be apprehended as a strategy to preserve journalistic authority, which has been decreasing over the past few decades (Carlson 2017). In the case of Ukraine, one interesting finding in our study is a partial shift away from the logic of speed and the inherent competition between media outlets. In the words of one of our sources: "Getting it right is more important than being the first".

Verification and source criticism can be tedious and time-consuming. In many ways it contradicts the fast pace of breaking news. Although "getting it right" was a statement echoed in several of our interviews, the claim was operationalized in several ways. In some news outlets, verification was established almost as a separate news genre focused on explaining the verification process behind false images or truth claims. Other newsrooms published imagery of uncertain origin using disclaimers, and sometimes fake images were reprinted as separate news stories because "they were already out there".

This chapter presents empirical findings from interviews with visual editors, news editors, foreign news editors, and photojournalists/multiskilled

DOI: 10.4324/9781003478072-4

reporters. It addresses how the influx of propaganda, disinformation, and misinformation from the war in Ukraine affected editorial processes in Norwegian and Swedish news outlets and how they have triggered new responses.

We have identified two strategies in how the news outlets in our sample deal with truth claims: The first is *presence in the field*, which is perceived to secure a truthful coverage of the social and political impact of the war (see Chapter 3 for further findings related to this). The second is *fact-checking* at the home desk, which supports a truthful rendering of facts from other sources.

Publishing unverified visuals or propaganda, unmasking it and relaying the news outlets' own (or that of other outlets) verification process, can also be seen as a way to maintain professional authority, according to respondents. From this angle, being on the ground in Ukraine may be considered a method of verification as well as a show of independence. When it comes to fact-checking on the home desk, we found two main approaches: one relying on classical journalistic source criticism and verification, resulting in a somewhat individualized and contingent approach. We refer to this strategy as "A hierarchy of trust". The other strategy is an investment in building skills in digital verification, drawing on so-called open-source intelligence (OSINT)[1] (or OSINF) sources. We refer to this strategy as "Skilling up". The presentation in the following is structured around these two strategies.

A hierarchy of trust

In-house teams traveling in the field were considered the most trustworthy, and their material was generally not verified by the home desk, according to respondents. As explained by one editor: "It's important to be able to see and verify, talk to sources and, over time, through increased familiarity, develop our own network of sources", echoing what others also articulated. One photojournalist explicitly made the connection between presence and verification, a position echoed by other photojournalists:

> Presence in the field equals showing the audience that we are here, we check, we know. The media's main capital is to be trusted by the audience, particularly in this situation where the sources of misinformation and disinformation are everywhere. And the most important aspect of trust is that the media can tell the audience: these are our people, our eyes, our ears.

Thus, to respondents, independent coverage includes having a presence on location. However, the importance of source criticism in the field, such as evaluating the effects of working in a foreign environment, within another language sphere, depending heavily on translators and fixers, was less problematized by editors and addressed mainly by respondents with field experience, such as this multiskilled reporter:

> Our contacts reflect our [personal and professional] networks. With time you get to know more people and you learn who to trust. Yet, we meet and interview people all the time with no idea of who they are. It's often difficult or impossible to verify all the details in the stories they tell.

Another respondent felt that editors put too much faith in their teams on assignment and spent too little time discussing the content they produced:

> It's like… they trust you because they know you, and then everybody else should also trust you. But this is too simplistic. I don't really understand the logic. It's like …I know my father, but I don't trust everything he says. There are always a thousand possible sources of error in a statement, even if it's said and believed with the best intentions. And sometimes, of course, the intentions are bad. Audiences are becoming more critical, and I think we have to be honest about these issues and engage with them.

One editor pointed out how the teams in the field could be compromised digitally: "Burner phones have become a colloquial term. We kill them with a nail after we have used them, but there is always the risk of being under surveillance and corrupted digitally. Any material we may have collected could be accessed by someone else".

Another concern raised was the prioritization of editorial resources on a long-term basis (also mentioned in Chapter 3):

> I think management has been reassured by our presence in the field and what we have been able to document with text and image in-between the rumors and all the unverified material. But this is a specialized profession with expertise that is built over the years. There are not that many of us, and it's important to understand that [our know-how] doesn't come out of nowhere.

Furthermore, the imagery produced by in-house photographers at an early stage of the conflict was found useful for verification purposes, some respondents said, including this editor, emphasizing the value of classical reporting routines at a time of desk reporting:

> The most important thing is always the same, that is to try to be there yourself on location with your team, to try to verify and do your own legwork. What happened? And how do we verify that? Well, by sending skilled journalists there. I always think that, whether it's an event in Ukraine or here at home, it doesn't really matter where it is. Journalistic legwork is

> best done on location. That's the only way you can be sure that what you're seeing is correct.

Relying on news agencies

National news agencies and other Western agencies (such as Reuters, AP, and AFP) were generally trusted and their material usually not verified, according to editors. As the main supplier of news photographs to the outlets, agencies represent quality and credibility to respondents. According to a tabloid news editor: "We trust and rely on the agencies. If we didn't, we couldn't do our job". However, at an early stage of the invasion, especially, some respondents said, the uncertainty about events made them withhold some imagery and delay certain stories until they could verify imagery as well as the story. One respondent said: "The point of departure is that we trust the agencies, but since propaganda images also can emerge there, [image publication] has to be an active choice on our part".

We found clear stages in the conflict corresponding to different challenges and strategies of verification in general. In the first few days of uncertainty following 24 February 2022, verification also had to do with finding out what was actually happening. This slowed publication of imagery in some newsrooms if it couldn't be ascertained, for example, whether the weaponry showed were Russian tanks crossing the border into Ukraine. One editor commented on the virality on social media as a pressure and a seemingly abundant source of usable visuals, which prompted readers to complain about the slow publication of stories about Ukraine:

> The first thing that struck us was that there were very few pictures coming in during the first week, and that makes the verification work more difficult. That's something we have not experienced before. We received criticism from readers that we were so slow to publish pictures...both pictures and information. And it was because we worked intensely with verification. On Twitter and such, you could find any number of pictures. But it turned out that much of it was not correct.

Less trusted sources

While in-house and agency presence represent the preferred sources in the hierarchy of trust, with little to no verification perceived to be needed, the multitude of other sources were considered less trustworthy. Official Russian and Ukrainian sources were considered inherently biased and were fact-checked when deemed necessary. The political dimensions, that is, the two countries' support of Ukraine, according to respondents, created a deeper suspicion against information from Russian sources. However, this was also attributed to the reality of the war—Russia's invasion of a sovereign neighboring state—and to years of Russian disinformation campaigns in Sweden and Norway and in other Western countries.[2] In the words of this respondent:

> But we're supposed to be skeptical and aware that they want to convey a favorable image of their side during the war. So absolutely, if you look at the media coverage in general it looks like that [biased]. But we work actively to ensure that we don't buy either party's narrative straight through, so verification is important on both sides.

One fact-checking specialist admitted that the pro-Ukrainian sentiment in the news coverage, as well as the public discourse, sometimes made it painful to reveal that Ukrainian soldiers also committed brutal acts against Russian soldiers during battle.

A lack of independently verified visual information from Russia-controlled areas was mentioned by respondents as a major concern, including by this editor discussing the coverage of the evacuation of Kherson in September 2023:

> Some news media ran with a disclaimer that they didn't know if it was a real evacuation or if it was staged…that it was staged and they [the Russians] had gathered a bunch of people and put them on buses to show the people of Kherson that it's time to leave. And those pictures are very hard to verify, I would say. And there's a great desire for those pictures. We want to show what we think we know. So, it's really tricky.

Third-party material

International agencies also provided the newsrooms with "third-party materials", signaling uncertainty about provenance or a lack of independence, such as Ukrainian government sources or other state-controlled media. In Sweden, the news agency TT, the main provider of international agency images to domestic news organizations, does not currently have a contract with the Russian government agency TASS.[3] However, some news outlets subscribe to the Russian agency independently. Several editors stressed the importance of relaying byline and provenance in the caption for the sake of transparency. In the words of this editor:

> If president Zelenskyy is visiting a site, there has to be a good reason for us to use a Ukrainian government handout image and not an agency photo. That story may also have doubtful news value, depending on the circumstances.

Social media played an important role as a source to public witnessing but with low or dubious credibility. One fact-checker referred to the war as a "TikTok war" because social media infiltrate everybody's lives, disregarding age:

> [The war] gets so close to everyone: children, youth, adults. There is so much content in social media, and this is difficult to verify. It comes into people's individual feeds for better or worse. Better because people are more informed about what's going on, worse because the media are misused.

The decision to publish social-media content also depended on the credibility of the source, if known. According to this editor:

> We might see a video posted to an X [Twitter] account we don't recognize, saying: "I filmed this from my bedroom window in Kyiv last night". That's really difficult to verify. We don't know who the person is. But if it's someone known to us, an organization or other news media, retweeting the video and saying: "This happened in Kyiv last night", then we know it has happened even if the person wasn't the one holding the camera [or smart-phone].

The speed of publication for the tabloid/breaking news-focused outlets sometimes resulted in publishing before completely verifying. In the words of this digital editor:

> The war is very scary and exciting, so to say, which we don't want to hide from our readers because we want to show what is happening. Then, it's important for us to publish the kind of materials where you can really see what is happening, because otherwise, if we were to wait for a "real" photographer, we might have to wait several days, or it may be too dangerous [for photographers] to go there.

Respondents also said that false visuals can make good stories, once they have been investigated. Some news editors asserted that they did publish unverified or false imagery, such as from X, justified as cases to be discussed as part of the news media's perceived duty to alert readers to propaganda in circulation on social media.

The influx of AI bots developing at a rapid pace was considered a new level of challenges to verification. According to this respondent: "This is a marathon, a double marathon. Verification will affect the rest of my working years". Another editor, in contrast, said: "I don't think I have been fooled yet". However, looking ahead to the near future, several editors said they worried that the news media are unprepared for how to handle AI in general. Photojournalists, in their interviews presented in the previous chapter, expressed strong concerns with AI technology. According to several photographers, a major concern with AI is how it raises doubts about the authenticity of all photographs, including the work of photojournalists.

Skilling up (digital forensics)

The conflict was described by respondents as a war of information in a rather intense way, which requires more knowledge and skills in news organizations, particularly with regard to images. According to one editor, the importance of verification reflects the value of photographs in journalism:

> Today, text is almost… of course it is not irrelevant, but it is less important for people's perceptions. There is no story without an image. […] In online media, the story leads only with the title and the image. And social media works in the same way, in many cases even without the title. […] This makes us very vulnerable to manipulation. Without the text, you also lose context. You lose the opportunity to explain beyond the moment. And the moment may deceive and give the wrong perspective, but it's really powerful.

One way of skilling up is OSINT, which has transcended from a fringe activity, performed by specialized investigative organizations such as Bellingcat, to a mainstream technique in most news media. OSINT combines analysis of visual metadata with geolocation, weather reports, face recognition, etc. This work is conducted from the home desk, and most newsrooms in our sample developed special expertise in this field, although only a few Swedish outlets have specialized in in-house verification desks. Even if the verification practices are similar, the approach differed significantly in the two countries.

Verification in Swedish newsrooms: individual approaches

Swedish respondents said that they were focusing more on verification in the coverage of Ukraine than previously and that they were spending more time doing it. Some described verification as relying mostly on the classical methods of establishing time, place, and event through knowledge about the events and the coverage. "Going by your gut feeling" was mentioned by several respondents, including this editor: "If something seems too good to be true, it probably is". In this respect, verification depends on individuals and their professional skills. Editors also said that they had developed routines to use some OSINT tools when needed, such as Google reverse image search, to check the first publication date of an image or to check an image in Photoshop.

Routines for image publication and support for digital editors were developed in the early part of the coverage, in initiatives such as verification tutorials held for staffers in one newsroom, and in adding rotating shifts for picture editors on weekends in newsrooms that normally don't have picture editors scheduled on evenings and weekends. One editor, interviewed in 2023, described a routine emerging out of skills learned in previous crises:

> We have a staffer who has set up a system for cases where we are unsure, if you want to check where an image is coming from, like we did during the attack at the airport in Brussels [in 2016]. So, we have routines for that. But we don't have a specific editorial project where we verify a large number of images. It's a specific image that you are unsure about or if you want to double check.

Several respondents said that the most common manipulation they found was related to time or place and not to manipulations within the image. SVT, the public-service television company, was the first Swedish news outlet to create a systematic visual verification initiative in response to disinformation in the war in Ukraine. "The Ukraine and Russia desk" was launched in late 2022, as explained by this respondent: "We came to a point where we realized that we need to get better at this". This respondent described the work as striving for an international level of skill needed for future coverage. With expertise in video reporting, Russian language skills, and foreign reporting, desk staffers have trained at Bellingcat, and they use a variety of tools similarly to their international counterparts. While the focus is on image verification, staffers also seek to broaden their pool of sources, such as using videos and tips from the messaging app Telegram to produce their own unique coverage. One example observed during the interview was a video circulating on X, said to show Ukrainians partying on a beach while the war raged. The desk's OSINT analysis found it to be false.

At the end of 2023, the Ukraine and Russia desk was renamed *SVT verifierar* and assigned to more broadly contribute to domestic and international coverage. A recent focus has been the war in Gaza after the Hamas attack on Israel on 7 October 2023. This broader focus also includes a pedagogical component to provide the public with verification and source criticism tools for visual materials.[4] The work of the desk has been integrated into television newscast reporting, and their methodology can be seen on the website svt.se where postings include their own reporting and the verification methods used. Recent examples include an entry disproving Russian claims that Swedish soldiers were fighting with their troops in Ukraine, the disinformation unmasked using OSINT methods. In another piece, the staff tested an AI tool scanning satellite visuals to assess the growth of Ukrainian cemeteries, adding new information about war-related casualties. In the past year, the work of the desk has been recognized by the Swedish organization of investigative journalists (FGJ).

In 2024, *Dagens Nyheter* launched its own verification desk consisting of staffers with picture editing, photojournalism, video, and social media publication skills. Interviewed shortly after their launch, respondents said their goal was, similarly to those of SVT, to work with image verification to support the news side, to unmask disinformation, and to be a resource for investigative journalism in the newsroom. Staffers also stressed the pedagogical focus to spread information about tools for verification and fact-checking, raising the level of skill in the newsroom and visual literacy among the public. Said one respondent: “It’s an unfamiliar feeling to look at the social-media visual stream and realize that now it’s up to us to verify, not the agencies”.

The *Dagens Nyheter* team has been attending a workshop and is currently trying out methods on projects while also starting to be on hand for verification queries. One area where the verification staff hopes to shift the focus is an internal mindset, to encourage considering images as documents to be interpreted: “Not in the sense of putting out disclaimers for pictures we’re uncertain about” but to state: “This is what we know, we know the *where*, but we don’t know the *who*”, an approach also described in interviews with staffers at SVT. According to the *Dagens Nyheter* respondents, the newsroom may miss out on stories by not pursuing information from social media and by being “cautious”, referring to an in-house policy to only use agency materials if it has been verified. The war in Ukraine was not perceived by these respondents as a direct catalyst for the initiative. Rather, from their experience, they viewed it as a response to the rising threat of AI, a concern mentioned by several editors as well as photojournalists in both countries (see further Chapter 3). The *Dagens Nyheter* respondents, like other editors, also said that credibility comes from a transparency achieved by sharing the methods used.

The Swedish newsrooms developed individual approaches to verify visual materials and information from the war in Ukraine. At the time of writing this chapter, two out of the five newsrooms, the public-service broadcast companies *SVT* and *Dagens Nyheter* have confirmed that they have launched verification desks, as discussed above. However, there have been previous initiatives. In the spring 2018, five Swedish media outlets launched a fact-checking collaboration to combat disinformation in the Swedish election in the fall of that year. With a shared site, the participants, which included public-service television and radio, along with *Dagens Nyheter*, *Svenska Dagbladet*, and the newspaper *Kit*, shared training and methodology. Each of the participating news outlets conducted their own fact-checking for their own stories (Allern & Pollack 2019, p. 286). The initiative was closed down at the beginning of 2019.

Norway: collaboration through Faktisk verifiserbar

In Norway, the leading media outlets settled for a collaborative approach based on the recognition of shared challenges and limited resources to handle them individually. In April 2022, the Norwegian public and private broadcasters NRK, TV 2, the Norwegian news agency NTB, the leading tabloids *VG* and *Dagbladet*, the main subscription outlet *Aftenposten*, and the small

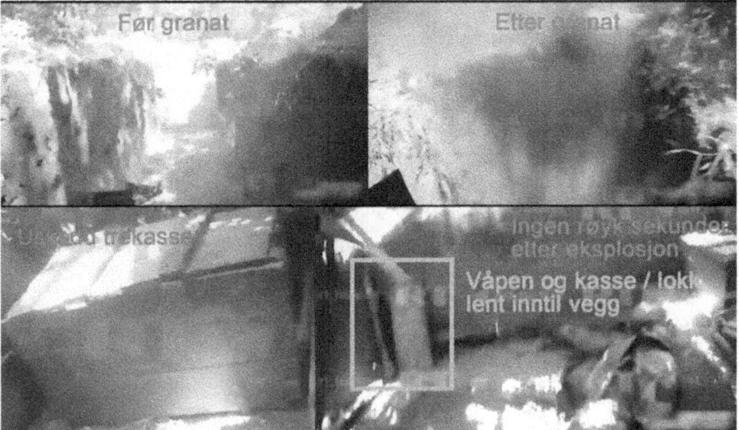

Figure 4.1 The screenshot shows discrepancies found by the verification team when verifying a Russian video disseminated on social media. The video allegedly showed an explosion supposed to have killed a Norwegian mercenary in Ukraine. Screenshot, *Faktisk verifiserbar*. Reproduced with permission.

national defense organ *Forsvarets Forum* joined forces in a unique partnership called *Faktisk verifiserbar*. The idea was born a couple of weeks after the invasion, when some of the leading editors met for a public debate on fake news from Ukraine at Pressens hus (House of the press) in Oslo. The idea of a shared verification hub was first suggested there (Andersen 2023). Some weeks later, at the yearly conference on investigative journalism (SKUP), the idea was detailed and, shortly thereafter, the first journalist moved into temporary locations in a bar under renovation in Pressens hus.

These details are important because they point to certain specifics about the Norwegian media ecology at this point. First, even if Norwegian news media are competitors in the media market, they also have a tradition of collaboration. Dating back to 1990, the foundation for investigative journalism (SKUP) was formed to promote excellence in investigative journalism across editorial boundaries. In 2017, *VG*, *Dagbladet*, NRK, TV 2, and the freedom-of-speech foundation Fritt Ord financially supported the launch of an independent fact-checking association, Faktisk.no, with the goal to promote "a fact-based dialogue and a constructive public debate".[5] In 2021, several media associations, such as the Norwegian journalist union, the Editors association, the Norwegian press association, and Faktisk.no, co-located at Pressens hus, a structure that also serves as a center for debate and education for the professional field. These initiatives provided a beneficial framework for the collaboration on fact-checking news from Ukraine. Second, the editors who instigated the initiative belong to the same generation and knew each other well. According to one informant, the element of interpersonal trust is not to be underestimated.

In the *Faktisk verifiserbar* project, reporters were trained to become verification specialists. As one of them put it: "We sat at Pressens hus and decided that we were going to get good at this. And everybody should contribute". The news media provided material they wanted to have examined, and whatever the team worked on was considered common property. As explained by this editor:

> The [fact-checking] capacity in the news media was scarce and dependent on a few enthusiasts. So, everybody understood that this war is too big for competition. [...] We could work together on [verification] and do our individual stuff in the field. [...] Everybody had something to gain from learning these things.

Practically, each entry was systematized in a verification database accessible to all. Every image or video was provided with an ID number and a document logging the results of the verification process. The team logged the coordinates of the material and, based on geolocation, found several images and videos from earlier wars e.g. Syria 2011–2019. They were also able to detect if an image originated from the site where it supposedly had been captured. Weather reports and other details helped in deciding on dates and the time of day and whether an image had been modified or not in Photoshop. Reverse image search was used to find out if an image had previously been published and face recognition tools to decide on a person's identity. The team also used their own AI software, designed to identify military vehicles.

In some cases, the imagery was clearly false. The alleged neo-Nazi Dalton Kennedy turned out to be an innocent Canadian who died in 2015. The smiling Russian paratrooper did his cheers during a training session a year before the war. In other cases, verification confirmed stories that later became breaking news e.g. that Russian missile carriages were heading north towards the Finnish border when Finland was discussing entering NATO and that strategic bomber planes were deployed 20 kilometers from the Norwegian border.[6]

Sometimes, however, the search was inconclusive, and at times the influx of images was too massive and the team had to prioritize. Close contact with organizations like Reuters or EBU (The European Broadcast Union) who also had strong verification departments helped in the selection process. If other fact-checkers were working on a specific case, the Norwegian team would often drop it. There are also examples of stories that were real, but that were not published because the visual material was too hard to verify. "Our work is very similar to the way the Intelligence services do it. It is a probability calculation", one fact-checker said.

Speed was a major challenge. The media often wanted results quicker than the verification team could provide. According to one fact-checker, a verification process can take between five minutes and several days, "but it's better to spend time and be certain than to publish quickly and be mistaken".

Photographers were underrepresented at the verification desk. One photojournalist was assigned by the home media outlet on a regular basis, and a few spent a day from time to time.[7] According to our informants, the work enhanced the participants' understanding of what images contain, what they tell, and how to interpret them, but it was not their impression that people with photographic background were better at this, even if their technical background was considered useful. As explained by one editor:

> In verification you see images in a completely different way. This has nothing to do with aesthetics. You look for shadows. Can the shadow tell you how tall a building is? Where is the sun, what does that say about the time of day? Did it rain on the day the image was supposedly taken? Where are the puddles?

This was a new way of thinking, and the project reached out to specialized groups, such as Center for Information Resilience and Bellingcat. The Norwegian Intelligence Service contributed with lectures on their methodology, including how to recognize objects from satellite imagery. As a nonprofit group, *Faktisk verifiserbar* even managed to get a deal with a satellite company themselves, which enabled them to do investigative work on their own.

One former editor stressed that the major ambition behind *Faktisk verifiserbar* was more than the verification of particular images. The most important task was building expertise in the media industry. The idea was that the people active at the verification desk later would enhance the expertise in their home media outlet and spread the methodology. One of his goals was to reduce the misconception that verification is only useful in investigative journalism:

> At the beginning [many editors believed] that what we needed were people with a heavy investigative background. But verification journalism is mostly journalism of the moment, in situations where each second counts. So […] it was very much a news desk, a breaking news group. We work with investigative tools and the methodology, but the pulse is different.

This was confirmed by a reporter who has later used verification tools in celebrity reporting with good results. "It's the mindset", the respondent said. "You get access to all kinds of information using these tools".

Some of the graphic imagery the team investigated turned out to be real depictions of dead bodies, mass graves, and even a case of live castration of a Ukrainian soldier. The project logged violent images and videos according to the degree of violence, but they discovered that they also needed a systematic approach to the effects these images had on the people working on them. In the words of one editor:

> We were sitting at this former bar, looking at the sunny streets of Oslo, while counting dead bodies in a mass grave, trying to identify dead faces, you know. There were some sick images at the start, and those images were real, so it was really unfiltered.

The desk established some general rules such as to avoid sitting alone with graphic material, to turn the sound down when looking at graphic footage, and maybe skid the faces of dead and wounded people: "It is impossible not to be marked by these images, and now, with Gaza, it is even worse. Several people who have former experiences with PTSD were retraumatized. [...] I had nightmares myself for a couple of months", one editor confessed and added that "this is not something you should do for many years in a row".[8]

The reporters assigned to the project later returned to their respective newsrooms, and the project was shut down in December 2022. This decision was controversial, as the initiative was considered highly successful, receiving national awards and international acclaim. According to one editor, the problem was money and the lack of staying power: "We are good at pulling together on a short-term basis, but when it came to establishing long-lasting structures, people withdrew".

However, the project was revived after 7 October 2023 and the start of the war in Gaza. At the time of writing, it has been integrated into the fact-checking website faktisk.no, strengthened with a couple of verification journalists from the NRK on temporary assignment. They now function more as an independent desk, doing their own stories, and free for any media to pick up or to build upon. They also continue to promote verification methodology. According to a former editor: "It is amazing how many journalists have never conducted a reverse image search. It's quite depressing, really".

Chapter summary: fact-checking as a new genre

We found a contrast between the two countries in their approach to how the up-skilling on OSINT methodology was organized as well as levels of up-skilling. Most respondents referred to verification as important, and most were wary of how to address future challenges related to AI technology. The question of how much the existing verification tools were used has more nuances. In the words of one editor: "I think we didn't quite understand what a resource this was. And we did some verification on our own, to a large degree based on our field experiences". Several respondents said that the most common manipulation they found was related to time or place and not to manipulations within the image.

In general, the expertise of picture editors was held up as becoming more important for verification purposes in this conflict. In newsrooms in both countries, topical skills and experience of staff photographers, reporters, such as foreign correspondents and Russian-speaking staffers, and investigative reporter colleagues were also mentioned as important resources that editors turned to. Editors working on the home desk also noted that their verification skills have grown over time as they become more knowledgeable about places and events in Ukraine and the circumstances and facts of the war.

Among the challenges for skilling up, noted by several respondents, were short deadlines and the pressure to publish quickly in digital media, a lack of resources and skills, such as Russian or Ukrainian language skills. There is also the issue of exclusivity and verification as a competitive strategy, expressed by this respondent:

> If we dedicate a lot of time to verifying something, or unmasking propaganda about something, then it has to be a really important story, and something the international outlets [such as AFP, Reuters, BBC or Bellingcat] haven't already fact-checked.

Another respondent expressed some frustration about the idea of fact-checking as the preferred way to solve problems with disinformation and misinformation:

> I think this is a temporary solution. It is expensive and almost impossible to upscale. In the media these days, they fire photojournalists and hire verification experts, but it doesn't really work in the long run, not with the obstacles ahead. We have to adopt another approach, stop running around looking for clues about what has already been produced and find a way to secure this information from the moment an image is captured.

Our findings show that it takes an allocation of resources and skills to build and maintain verification expertise. The organization and relationship between different media and individuals may help explain whether individual or collaborative approaches develop, for instance, the different strategies in the two countries.

Within the newsroom, internal factors and routines also have an impact on the development of fact-checking skills. A newsroom study conducted in Sweden prior to the Russian invasion of Ukraine found that staff training and the implementation of new fact-checking routines stalled, attributed to a lack of resources and also to a hesitation about implementing a new workflow (Picha Edwardsson et al. 2021). This, in turn, was attributed by the scholars to the pressure to deliver news fast. This challenge was echoed by our respondents, specifically regarding the apparent contradiction between the pace of news (=fast) and fact-checking (=slow). Another recent study, also conducted in Sweden, examined fact-checking of information in stories out of Ukraine. Editors were found to use "disclaimers" as a way to publish while also signaling an uncertain provenance, in effect leaving the fact-checking job to readers (Nygren & Widholm 2022).

Respondents quoted in this chapter as well as Chapter 3 confirmed that they are aware of a trust gap in the current broader media culture. Verification has been held up by our respondents and in the literature, as a strategy for journalists to build trust (Carlson 2017; Jukes 2022; Steensen et al. 2022; Waisbord 2018).

Notes

1 Open Source Intelligence /Information.
2 https://www.theguardian.com/world/article/2024/aug/29/sweden-warns-of-heightened-risk-of-russian-sabotage
3 TT Chief of photography, personal communication
4 Media interview with SVT Head of News https://www.dagensmedia.se/medier/rorligt/svts-nya-satsningar-verifiera-barn-och-vetenskap/
5 https://www.faktisk.no/om-oss
6 https://www.faktisk.no/artikler/z25lo/satellittbilder-viser-11-strategiske-bombefly-20-mil-fra-norge
7 In the second round of the project, there have been more, both photojournalists and multiskilled reporters.
8 While research has addressed PTSD among journalists in the field covering crises, research has also found a potentially traumatic impact on editors tasked with viewing explicit and violent visual content. See for example Feinstein, A., Audet, B., & Waknine, E. (2014). Witnessing Images of Extreme Violence: A Psychological Study of Journalists in the Newsroom. *JRSM Open,* 5(8), 2–7.

5 Reflections on the Norwegian and Swedish visual coverage of the war in Ukraine

Our aim with this book was to explore visual meaning-making and witnessing in the news coverage of the war in Ukraine. Empirically, we conducted a study of ten Norwegian and Swedish news outlets covering the conflict, focusing on differently sourced and produced visually driven stories at different points in time, how journalists negotiated their position as gatekeepers and witnesses, and how the newsrooms handled imagery in this "information war" in order to ascertain truth and falsehoods. In this chapter, we reflect on the findings from our study and discuss broader implications, about how journalism is equipped to handle the influx of propaganda and disinformation, and the position of international reporting at a time of dwindling resources in the media sector.

In our first empirical chapter, Chapter 2, we explored witnessing through journalism as a bridge between the news event and the distant audience, specifically by analyzing imagery at three points in time. Here, we used established methods in a new context of visual flows, by introducing a multifaceted approach theorized by Henning (2018). Specifically, we empirically applied Henning's notions of the digital image flow "jarring, jagged and disruptive" (ibid, p.142), which should be treated "as a temporary articulation, an arrangement that will shift and change" (ibid, p. 143) rather than a fixed entity.

Our aim was to make a methodological contribution to the field. Our conclusion is that established visual theory is still relevant but needs to be complemented by new methods to study the multi-source, multi-platform, and varied forms of visually driven information in the news media. We also sought to contribute theoretically to an area within journalism and media research where the single image remains a focus of empirical research. In our view, this focus misses the visual flows that also appear in the news. Furthermore, the single image no longer stands alone. In our analysis of visuals during the first two weeks of the full-scale Russian invasion, we could confirm this by conducting a close reading of the coverage, collectively reading several hundred stories. By placing ourselves in the position of media consumers (which we are), looking at video clips, gifs, photographs, videos, and social-media entries embedded in other forms of journalistic content, we sought to simulate

DOI: 10.4324/9781003478072-5

the experience of being exposed to flow. Of course, we realize that following a flow by opening separate stories on the search engine we used is not the same as taking in news and other information in real time on digital sites, but this was as close as we could get in our research conducted retrospectively.

Yet the images deserve scrutiny. Bridges and flows, our chapter title, refer to how editors at the home desk sought to bridge the distance between events on the ground and visuals emanating from there and audiences at home. Our findings in the first part of the chapter show that editors, beyond the visual news flow from agencies and other sources, used storytelling along an axis of proximity and distance, where proximity is the mode most appealing to audiences. This suggests that the growth in illustrative photography in the field of photojournalism (Fabregat 2013; Vobič & Trivundža 2015), shifting from indexical-iconic visual communication to metaphorical visual communication, is counter to audience preferences.

In the next part of the chapter, in an exploration of witnessing through journalism in the stories about Bucha and Borodyanka in April 2022, we applied the concept of visibility to analyze how the victims and survivors of the massacres were visualized. While the visuals during the first two weeks were mostly sourced from agencies and social media as the news outlets had to evacuate or were not yet on location in Ukraine, the coverage was focused and the news outlets relied on professional photographers, including their own teams. While the Scandinavian outlets covered several liberated towns, it was Bucha that came to symbolize Russian cruelty, lending the images from there a metonymic quality.

Our exploration of metonymy continued in the final part of the chapter, where we looked at how visual tropes and figures were articulated in commemorative stories published at the one-year mark, 24 February 2023. We found (almost surprisingly) few iconic images, a sign that iconicity is not as pronounced in the digital news presentation (Hariman & Lucaites 2018). We also found nuanced visualizations positioned as memorable. In this respect, our findings diverge from the literature on framing and witnessing identifying an othered portrayal in the coverage (Chouliaraki & Stolic 2017; Griffin 2010; Parry 2010). We attribute the contrast to the specific context of Ukraine where, to the Scandinavian news outlets and the public at home, the Ukrainians were seen as "people just like us", a sentiment also expressed in our interviews. Furthermore, we believe that in-depth coverage, such as that produced by these outlets, may offer opportunities for storytelling that is not possible in the singular image. While we don't suggest that a single photograph is inherently a stereotypical representation, the task of expressing a complex story in one image (such as the cover photo of a print-edition newspaper), necessitates a narrower topical and visual focus than a reportage. Another possible factor is that, as several outlets had conducted in-house coverage from Ukraine during 2022 and the conflict had been covered extensively by agencies, editors had extensive visual materials to choose from.

In Chapter 3, we continued our examination of witnessing, through findings from our interviews with 28 editors and 8 photojournalists focusing on their experiences covering Ukraine. The interviews contributed a real-time perspective of the coverage of an ongoing conflict, which we believe was of significant value for the study. Using gatekeeping as our concept, we looked at aspects of routines and witnessing and how they were affected in the coverage of this conflict. We identified three salient themes: being on location and keeping the public at home engaged, witnessing and showing the human cost of war, and handling access and bias.

Being on location was considered by respondents to be an assertion of quality, veracity and proximity, and a way to engage readers. We found that the photojournalists interviewed balanced the demands of assignments and digital publishing with a desire to find unique angles to keep the public engaged. While most editors said their newsrooms had placed increased resources to cover this important story and the visual area had raised its status (Nilsson 2021), some mainly conducted desk reporting, the most common form of international coverage by Scandinavian news outlets (Nygren & Widholm 2022).

Publishing photos of victims of the war was seen as less controversial in this conflict than others, although editors said they published more explicit visual content than they would do otherwise, attributed to a moral position but also, we deduced, from the lack of controversy and polarization in Norwegian and Swedish society about the politics of this conflict. Interestingly, we did not find a marked difference between editors and photojournalists who were at the scene and close to people affected. As a result, we found that respondents asserted their role as gatekeepers in the selection of images from the war.

Bias and "patriotic journalism" (Nygren & Widholm 2024; Ojala & Pantti 2017) were acknowledged by respondents and attributed to a lack of access to and trust in Russian-sourced information and also as a blind spot among the news media (Bergman & Hearns-Branaman 2024; Nygren & Widholm 2024).

The question of trust and credibility engaged the photojournalist respondents in particular. The rise of generative AI, in the past year in particular, was perceived as a threat to the credibility of their work since all images could be considered "fake" or questionable, in the eyes of the public. In the context of this discussion, respondents asserted that photojournalists have an increased responsibility today to earn the trust of the public, through transparency and ethics. The control of information, more broadly than the war in Ukraine, caused editors to voice concern over its impact on visual quality: fewer or embedded visual sources leading to less variety and the risk of reporters becoming targets in the conflict.

The experience of the respondents raises questions about whether international reporting is a prioritized area to news organizations, specifically in Scandinavia, but perhaps also in other regions. From our interviews, we gleaned that it is not necessarily about who is photographing, but rather that it takes time to build skills in foreign reporting and not all newsrooms had those skills or resources at the onset of the invasion. Photojournalism has been valued in the current coverage and the coverage has been of high quality. However, as a sign of precarity, some newsrooms have few in-house resources to conduct the coverage. Furthermore, by contracting for stories rather than hiring, journalists may not be able to make a long-term commitment to the profession. When on assignment, freelancers may also feel or actually be more exposed. This vulnerability has been noted in studies on freelancers and the "precarity" of photojournalism as a profession, which has been found to have a negative impact on the quality of news coverage (e.g. Caple 2019; Palmer 2022; Røe Mathisen, 2017). Our interviews also showed the speed of changes in journalism, where functions and roles are redefined, disappear, or are replaced by new areas of focus requiring new fields of expertise (Caple 2019; Simonsen & Evensen 2017; Nilsson 2021). We also noticed that concerns with AI emerged more in our later interviews (in 2024), while it was barely mentioned in interviews conducted in 2023, a sign of the rapid development of new technologies that require journalists to adapt.

In the fourth and final empirical chapter, we explored routines for visual verification in the newsrooms. In this part of the study, based on findings from our interviews, we identified two strategies. In one strategy, which we call a hierarchy of trust, editors verified visuals based on routines, where the most trusted—staff reporting—was generally not verified. On the next level down, news agency content was generally considered credible, and editors relied on the verification of these suppliers, as one editor said: "If we didn't trust the agencies, we couldn't do our job". However, the agencies can also be wrong, especially if they supply third-party content, leading editors to fact-check agency visuals as needed, in particular during the breaking-news phase of the invasion. The less credible sources, third-party materials from government sources (Ukrainian or Russian sources), social media or private sources were considered less credible (Chouliaraki & Al-Ghazzi 2022). Images with uncertain provenance were in some cases published along with a "disclaimer" found in previous research about fact-checking information in this war (Nygren & Widholm 2022).

The other strategy, skilling-up, developed in response to the disinformation reverberating in this "war of information" (Mortensen & Pantti 2023). In these initiatives, following approaches used by international outlets, editors used OSINT tools to identify source and other information about visuals and other content. In this work, AI was seen both as a threat—as part of disinformation—and as a tool in the verification process. The news outlets in the two countries developed different strategies. In Norway, a collaborative initiative built a newsroom with OSINT expertise servicing all Norwegian news media, with the expressed intent to pass on skills and build know-how as a collective. In Sweden, two news outlets developed their own internal visual verification desks during this conflict, Swedish public-service television in late 2022, and *Dagens Nyheter* in 2024. In contrast to the Norwegian *Faktisk verifiserbar*, the Swedish verification desks were in-house initiatives serving one newsroom. While several interview respondents considered it necessary to "skill-up", the long-term commitment to these initiatives is not certain at the time of writing this book. However, as has been noted in the literature, verification and fact-checking have been adopted by the news media as a way to assert and build trust with the public (Jukes 2022; Steensen et al. 2022) and, crucially, to confront disinformation. However, research has also found that a lack of long-term commitment and resources may be obstacles to the implementation (Picha Edwardsson et al. 2021). Our respondents found it a challenge to decide what to focus on given the resources needed, and some found the task overwhelming given the wealth of disinformation. Thus, it appears that clear strategies as well as resources are needed. Fact-checking could be seen as service to the public and a way for journalism to build and, perhaps, regain trust and also as a competitive approach and a kind of branding.

While our study does not focus specifically on boundary work, there are various aspects of boundaries that emerge in our findings. The boundary between the still image and moving images dissolves and blurs in the visual streams. Speaking with Henning, it may be "ever more necessary to pause and practice different kinds of reading" (2018, p. 143). The roles in news organizations are changing at a rapid pace, which we also found happened in newsrooms during the course of our study, yet another sign of blurred and shifting boundaries within the profession. Boundaries between citizen image-makers and journalists were also negotiated, in ethical deliberations about photographs and in processes of fact-checking and verification. Through the verification routines at the home desk, editors strived to set boundaries between true and false. However, as our respondents noted and as the literature notes (Steensen et al. 2022; Waisbord 2018), verification is an interpretative process, which, when applied to visuals, may result in: "We know X and Y, but we are not sure about Z". While this can be expressed in words in an article, that is not the case in an image which, according to cultural perceptions of the news photograph, is expected to depict events truthfully. The other related aspect of boundaries for verification and fact-checking is that the journalists asserted "trust" as a factor of credibility that has to be earned through transparency.

Our findings, pertaining to the routines and strategies of ten Scandinavian news outlets covering this modern war, raise a set of questions that point to the need for future research.

We found that journalists are still gatekeepers negotiating with other actors. We also found that trust and credibility are perceived as challenges and as a strategy to maintain and strengthen the position of journalism. Furthermore, verification is a competitive edge and an assertion of quality, though it is an emerging practice with an uncertain trajectory.

The specific findings from the newsrooms, in the new initiatives for visual verification and fact-checking, are interesting signs that news outlets are taking disinformation seriously. However, it's uncertain whether and, if so, how they will develop. Cultural contrasts appeared to be one factor in the different strategies between Norway and Sweden, where Norway has a tradition of collegial and professional cooperation with roots in investigative journalism networks and other initiatives. Sweden also has a history of fact-checking initiatives, such as Viralgranskaren, an early initiative in the Nordic region (Allern & Pollack, 2019, p. 286), founded in 2014 by the newspaper *Metro*, and the aforementioned 2018 initiative. These emerging initiatives in Scandinavia, modeled on international networks and actors, started in response to the challenges of disinformation.

While it is beyond the scope of our study to analyze the work of these initiatives, more research is needed, not just to evaluate but to assist news organizations in this task, in line with previous research. Also needed, according to respondents, is more research on AI, as a tool and a challenge for journalism and, more broadly of course, for the public.

Respondents also addressed the control of information, not as a new challenge but as an obstacle to independent journalism. Small outlets in a small media market like Norway and Sweden find value in being on location which, apparently, the public does as well. The questions of future strategies on this point are also outside the scope of this study. Yet, our findings raise questions about the sustainability of foreign reporting. In part, this is due to the rapid changes in the journalistic field that make the profession and the practice a moving target. In part, as noted, it is also dependent on the resources and strategies of the news organizations.

References

Allan, S. (2014). Witnessing in Crisis: Photo Reportage of Terror Attacks in Boston and London. *Media, War & Conflict,* 7(2): 133–151.

Allan, S., & Zelizer, B. (2004). *Reporting War: Journalism in Wartime.* Routledge.

Allern, S., & Pollack, E. (2017). Journalism as a Public Good: A Scandinavian Perspective. *Journalism,* 20(11): 1423–1439.

Allern, S., & Pollack, E. (2019). *Källkritik: journalistik i lögnens tid.* Studentlitteratur.

Andén-Papadopoulos, K., & Pantti, M. (2013). Re-imaging Crisis Reporting: Professional Ideology of Journalists and Citizen Images. *Journalism,* 14(7): 960–977.

Andersen, I. (2023). *Tracing truth: how journalists in faktisk verifiserbar used digital technologies to verify information from the warzone in Ukraine.* Master dissertation. University of Oslo.

Azoulay, A. (2012). *The Civil Contract of Photography.* Zone Books.

Balan, J. (2022). Why Did Russia Invade Ukraine? FAQs about the Conflict That Has Shocked the World. *The Conversation.* Downloaded on 16 November, 2024. https://theconversation.com/why-did-russia-invade-ukraine-faqs-about-the-conflict-that-has-shocked-the-world-177963

Barthel, M., & Burkner, H-J. (2019). Ukraine and the Big Moral Divide. What Biased Media Coverage Means to East European Border. *Geopolitics,* 25(3): 633–657.

Barthes, R. (2000). *Camera Lucida:* Reflections on Photography. Vintage.

Barthes, R. (1977). *Image, Music, Text.* Fontana.

Bergman, T., & Hearns-Branaman, J.O. (2024). *Media, Dissidence and the War in Ukraine.* Routledge.

Bjerknes, F. (2022). Images of Transgressions: Visuals as Reconstructed Evidence in Digital Investigative Journalism. *Journalism Studies,* 23(8): 951–973.

Bjerknes, F. (2012). Rett sted til rett tid: En studie av hvordan visuell ledelse og ulike måter å organisere en fotoavdeling på influerer den visuelle journalistikken i to aviser. Master dissertation. University of Oslo.

Blakely, A., & Lloyd, D. (2021). Photojournalism and Documentary Practice: When Sometimes We Turn Away. *Social Alternatives,* 40(2): 6–14.

Boyko, K., & Horbyk, R. (2023). Swarm Communication in a Totalizing War: Media Infrastructures, Actors and Practices in Ukraine during the 2022 Russian Invasion. In Mortensen, M. & Pantti, M. (Eds.), *Media and the War in Ukraine* (pp. 37–56). Peter Lang.

Brothers, C. (1997). *War and Photography.* Routledge.

Bruun, H., & Münter Lassen, J. (2024). Pushing Public Service Television Online: A Quantitative Study of the Cross-promotional Continuity Announcements on DR and TV 2 Denmark. *Norsk medietidsskrift*, 31(1): 1–16.

Capilla, P. (2021). Post-truth as a Mutation of Epistemology in Journalism. *Media and Communication*, 9(1): 313–322.

Caple, H. (2019). *Photojournalism Disrupted: The View from Australia*. Routledge.

Caple, H., & Bednarek, M. (2016). News Values: What a Discursive Approach Can Tell Us about the Construction of News Discourse and News Photography. *Journalism*, 17(4): 435–455.

Carlson, M. (2017). *Journalistic Authority: Legitimating News in the Digital Era*. Columbia University Press.

Carlson, M. (2019). News Algorithms, Photojournalism and the Assumption of Mechanical Objectivity in Journalism. *Digital Journalism*, 7(8): 1117–1133.

Chouliaraki, L. (2007). *The Spectatorship of Suffering*. Sage.

Chouliaraki, L. (2009). Witnessing War: Economies of Regulation in Reporting War and Conflict. *The Communication Review*, 12(3): 215–226.

Chouliaraki, L., & Al-Ghazzi, O. (2022). Beyond Verification: Flesh Witnessing and the Significance of Embodiment in Conflict News. *Journalism*, 23(3): 649–667.

Chouliaraki, L., & Stolic, T. (2017). Rethinking Media Responsibility in the Refugee 'Crisis': A Visual Typology of European News. *Media, Culture & Society*, 39(8): 1162–1177.

Eide, E., & Simonsen, A.H. (2007). *Mistenkelige utlendinger. Minoriteter i norsk presse gjennom hundre år*. Høyskoleforlaget.

Eide, E., & Simonsen, A.H. (2008). *Verden skapes hjemmefra. Pressedekningen av den ikke-vestlige verden 1902–2002*. Unipub.

Evensen, J.P., & Simonsen, A.H. (2019). *Se! Lærebok i visuell journalistikk*. Cappelen Damm akademisk.

Fabregat, H.D. (2013). La Manipulación de la Imagen Informativa. Retos y Oportunidades Para el Fotoperiodismo en el Contexto Digital. *Sphera Pública*, 2(13): 106–123.

Fahmy, S., Bock, M.A., & Wanta, W. (2014). *Visual Communication Theory and Research: A Mass Communication Perspective*. Palgrave Macmillan.

Fahmy, S., & Kim, D. (2008). Picturing the Iraq War: Constructing the Image of War in the British and US Press. *International Communication Gazette*, 70(6): 443–462.

Ferrucci P., Taylor, R., & Alaimoet, K.I. (2020). On the Boundaries: Professional Photojournalists Navigating Identity in an Age of Technological Democratization. *Digital Journalism*, 8(3): 367–385.

Fonn, B.K. (2015). *50 år med journalistutdanning: en historie om akademiseringen av et yrkesfag*. Cappelen Damm akademisk.

Frosh, P. (2011). Phatic Morality: Television and Proper Distance- *International Journal of Cultural Studies*, 14(4): 383–400.

Frosh, P., & Pinchevski, A. (2014). Media Witnessing and the Ripeness of Time. *Cultural Studies*, 28(4): 594–610.

Fürsich, E. (2010). Media and the Representation of Others. *International Social Science Journal*, 61(199): 113–130.

Galtung, J., & Ruge, M. (1965). The Structure of Foreign News. *Journal of Peace Research*, 1: 64–91.

Ghersetti, M., & Johansson, B. (2021). To Publish or Not to Publish: Assessing Journalism Ethics in News about a Terrorist Attack. *Journalism Studies*, 22(13): 1814–1831.

Greenwood, K., & Jenkins, J. (2015). Visual Framing of the Syrian Conflict in News and Public Affairs Magazines. *Journalism Studies,* 16(2): 207–227.

Griffin, M. (2010. Media Images of war. *Media, War & Conflict,* 3(1): 7–41.

Griffin, M., & Lee, J. (1995). Picturing the Gulf War: Constructing and Image of War in Time, Newsweek, and U.S. News & World Report. *Journalism & Mass Communication Quarterly,* 72(4): 813–825.

Gürsel, Z.D. (2016). *Image Brokers: Visualizing World News in the Age of Digital Circulation.* University of California Press.

Gynnild, A. (2017). The Visual Power of News Agencies. *Nordicom Review, 38*(2): 25–39.

Gynnild, A., Nilsson, M., Simonsen, A.H., & Weselius, H. (2017). Introduction. Photojournalism and Editorial Processes. *Nordicom Review,* 38(2): 1–5.

Hagan, S.M. (2023). *The Space Between Look and Read.* MIT Press.

Hagan, S.M. (2007). Visual/verbal Collaboration in Print: Complementary Differences, Necessary Ties, and an Untapped Rhetorical Opportunity. *Written Communication,* 24(1): 49–83.

Hahn, O., & Stalph, F. (2018). *Digital Investigative Journalism: Data, Visual Analytics and Innovative Methodologies in International Reporting.* Springer International.

Hall, S. (2009). Encoding/decoding. In Thornham, S., Basset, C. & Marris, P. (Eds.), *Media Studies: A Reader* (pp. 28–38). Edinburgh University Press.

Hanusch, F. (2012). The Visibility of Disaster Death in News Images. A Comparison of Newspapers from 15 Countries. *The International Communication Gazette,* 74(7): 655–672.

Harcup, T., & O'Neill, D. (2017). What Is News? News Values Revisited (Again). *Journalism Studies,* 18(12): 1470–1488.

Hariman, R., & Lucaites, J.L. (2007). *No Caption Needed: Iconic Photographs, Public Culture, and Liberal Democracy.* University of Chicago Press.

Hariman, R., & Lucaites, J.L. (2018). Predicting the Present: Iconic Photographs and Public Culture in the Digital Media Environment, *Journalism & Communication Monographs,* 20 (4): 318–324.

Hariman, R., & Lucaites, J.L. (2016). *The Public Image: Photography and Civic Spectatorship.* University of Chicago Press.

Henning, M. (2018). Image Flow. Photography on Tap. *Photographies,* 11(2-3): 133–148.

Ireton, C., & Posetti, J. (2018). *Journalism, Fake News & Disinformation: Handbook for Journalism Education and Training.* UNESCO series on journalism education.

Jukes, S. (2022). *News Agencies: Anachronism or Lifeblood of the Media System?* Routledge.

Khan, S.A., Sheiki, G., Opdahl, A.L., Rabbi, F., Stoppel, S., Trattner, C., & Dang-Nguyen, D. (2023). Visual User-generated Content Verification in Journalism: An Overview. *IEEE Access,* 11: 1–1.

Kot, S., Mozolevska, A., & Polischuk, O. (2024). Digital War Diaries: Witnessing the 2022 Russian War against Ukraine. *Memory, Mind & Media,* 3, article e15.

Kress, G., & Van Leeuwen, T. (2006). *Reading Images: The Grammar of Visual Design.* Routledge.

Linfield, S. (2010). *The Cruel Radiance: Photography and Political Violence.* The University of Chicago Press.

Lister, M. (2013). *The Photographic Image in Digital Culture* (second edition). Routledge.

Merrill, S. (2023). Memory, Iconicity, and Virality in Action: Exploring Protest Photos Online. In Rigney, A. & Smits, T. (Eds.), *The Visual Memory of Protest* (pp. 133–156). Amsterdam University Press.

Mitchell, W.J.T. (2005). There Are No Visual Media. *Journal of Visual Culture*, 4(2): 257–266.

Mitchell, W.J.T. (2002). Showing Seeing: A Critique of Visual Culture. *Journal of Visual Culture*, 1(2): 165–181.

Mitchell, W.J.T. (2007). *What Do Pictures Want?: The Lives and Loves of Images*. University of Chicago Press.

Mitchell, W. J. T. (1994) *Picture Theory. Essays on Verbal and Visual Representation*. University of Chicago Press.

Moriarty, S., & Shaw, D. (1995). An Antiseptic War: Were News Magazines of the Gulf War Too Soft? *Visual Communication Quarterly*, 2(2): 4–8.

Morse, T. (2014). Covering the Dead. *Journalism Studies,* 15(1): 98–113.

Mortensen. (2016). The Image Speaks for Iself"–or Does It? Instant News Icons, Impromptu Publics, and the 2015 European "Refugee crisis". *Communication and the Public*, 1(4): 409–422.

Mortensen, M., Allan, S., & Peters, C. (2017). The Iconic Image in a Digital Age: Editorial Mediations over the Alan Kurdi Photographs. *Nordicom Review,* 38(2): 71–86.

Mortensen, T. & Keshelasvili, A. (2013): If Everyone with a Camera Can Do This, Then What? Professional Photojournalists' Sense of Professional Threat in the Face of Citizen Photojournalism. *Visual Communication Quarterly*, 20(3): 144–158.

Mortensen, M., & Pantti, M. (Eds.) (2023). *Media and the War in Ukraine.* Peter Lang.

Moses, M. (2000). Consumer Mentality. *American Editor*, 808: 6–7.

Muindi, B. (2023). Psychological and Physical Lived Experiences of Journalists Covering Terrorism in Kenya. *Journalism & Mass Communication Educator*, 78(2): 251–266.

Murrell, C. (2015). *Foreign Correspondents and International Newsgathering: The Role of Fixers*. Routledge.

Naas, M. (2011). *The Truth in Photography*. Edinburgh University Press.

Newton, J. (2001). *The Burden of Visual Truth: The Role of Photojournalism in Mediating Reality.* Lawrence Erlbaum Associates.

Nilsson, M. (2019). An Ethics of (Not) Showing: Citizen Witnessing, Journalism and Visualizations of a Terror Attack. *Journalism Practice*, 14(3): 259–276.

Nilsson, M. (2021). Expendable or Valuable? Photojournalism in Five Swedish Newspapers Affected by Organizational Changes. *Journalistica,* 15(1): 33–58.

Nilsson, M. (2022). Nyhetsbilden berättar och provocerar. I *Källkritik och krig—propaganda, desinformation och lögner* (pp. 97–107). Institutet för mediestudier.

Nilsson, M., & Wadbring, I. (2015). Not Good Enough? Amateur Images in the Regular News Flow of Print and Online Newspapers. *Journalism Practice,* 9(4): 484–501.

Nygren, G., Glowacki, M., Hök, J., Kiria, I., Orlova, D., & Taradai, D. (2018). Journalism in the Crossfire: Media Coverage of the War in Ukraine in 2014. *Journalism Studies,* 19(7): 1059–1078.

Nygren, G., & Widholm, A. (2022). Hur vet medierna? Källkritik och desinformation i bevakningen av kriget i Ukraina. I *Källkritik & krig: Propaganda, desinformation och lögner* (pp. 13–73). Institutet för Mediestudier.

Nygren, G., & Widholm, A. (2024). *Informationskrigets nya vägar: Sociala medier, krigsrapportering och desinformation.* Södertörns högskola och Stockholms universitet. https://www.diva-portal.org/smash/get/diva2:1842606/FULLTEXT01.pdf

Ojala, M., & Pantti, M. (2017). Naturalizing the Cold War: The Geopolitics of Framing the Ukrainian Conflict in Four European Eewspapers. *Global Media & Communication,* 13(1): 41–56.

Olsson, E. (2010). Defining Crisis News Events: How News Organization Managers Drew upon History When Handling the Terror Attacks of September 11. *Nordicom Review,* 31(1): 87–102.

Palmer, L (2019). *The Fixers: Local News Workers and the Underground Labor of International Reporting.* Oxford University Press.

Palmer, L. (2022). The Precarious Labor of Freelance War Correspondents. In Chada, K. & Steiner, L. (Eds.), *Newswork and Precarity* (pp. 84–96). Taylor & Francis E-books.

Parry, K. (2010). Images of Liberation: Visual Framing, Humanitarianism and British Press Photography during the 2003 Iraq Invasion. *Media, Culture & Society,* 33(8): 1185–1201.

Patrick, C., & Allan, S. (2013). The Camera as Witness: The Changing Nature of Photojournalism. In Fowler- Watt, K. & Allan, S. (Eds.), *Journalism: New Challenges* (pp. 162–184). Centre for Journalism & Communication Research, Bournemouth University.

Picha Edwardsson, M., Al-Saqaf, W., & Nygren, G. (2021). Verification of Digital Sources in Swedish Newsrooms—A Technical Issue or a Question of Newsroom Culture? *Journalism Practice,* 17(8): 1678–1695.

Proitz, L. (2018). Visual Social Media and Affectivity: The Impact of the Image of Alan Kurdi and Young People's Response to the Refugee Crisis in Oslo and Sheffield. *Information, Communication & Society*, 21(4): 548–563.

Røe Mathisen, B. (2017). Entrepreneurs and Idealists: Freelance Journalists at the Intersection of Autonomy and Constraints. *Journalism Practice*, 11(7): 909–924.

Røe Mathisen, B. (2023). *Journalism between Disruption and Resilience*. Routledge.

Rose, G. (2023). *Visual Methodologies: An Introduction to Researching with Visual Materials*. Sage.

Rubinstein, D., & Sluis, K. (2013). Notes on the Margins of Metadata: Concerning the Undecidability of the Digital Image. *Photographies,* 6(1): 151–158.

Schwalbe, C.B., Silcock, W.B., & Candello, E. (2015). Gatecheckers at the Visual News Stream. *Journalism Practice,* 9(4): 465–483.

Seyser, D., & Zeiller, M. (2018). Scrollytelling - An Analysis of Visual Storytelling in Online Journalism. Conference proceedings, *22nd International Conference Information Visualisation* (IV), pp. 401–406.

Shoemaker, P.J., & Vos, T.P. (2009). Gatekeeping Theory. Routledge.

Simonsen, A.H. (2015). *Tragediens bilder. Et prosessuelt perspektiv på nyhetsbilder fra 22. juli.* Doctoral dissertation, University of Bergen.

Simonsen, A. H. & Evensen, J. P. (2017). Crisis, What Crisis? Three Nordic Photo Departments Fighting Back. Nordicom Review, 38(2): 87–102.

Skovholt, K., & Veum, A. (2022). *Tekstanalyse – ei innføring.* Cappelen Damm akademisk.

Sliwinski, S. (2011). *Human Rights in Camera.* University of Chicago Press.

Somerstein, R. (2020). 'Stay Back for Your Own Safety': News Photographers, Interference, and the Photographs They Are Prevented from Taking. *Journalism,* 21(6): 746–765.

Sontag, S. (1978). *On Photography*. Lane.

Steensen, S., Belair-Gagnon, V., Graves, L., Kalsnes, B., & Westlund, O. (2022). Journalism and Source Criticism. Revised Approaches to Assessing Truth-Claims. *Journalism Studies*, 23(16): 2119–2137.

Sturken, M., & Cartwright, L. (2018). *Practices of Looking: An Introduction to Visual Culture*. Oxford University Press.

Thomson, T.J., Angus, D., Dootson, P., Hurcombe, E., & Smith, A. (2022). Visual Mis/disinformation in Journalism and Public Communications: Current Verification Practices, Challenges, and Future Opportunities. *Journalism Practice*, 16(5): 938–962.

Usher, N. (2009). Recovery from Disaster: How Journalists at the New Orleans Times Picayune Understand the Role of a Post-Katrina Newspaper. *Journalism Practice*, 3(2): 216–132.

Van Leeuwen, T. (2020). Multimodality and Multimodal rRsearch. In Pauwels, L. & Mannay, D. (Eds.), *The Sage Handbook of Visual Research Methods* (pp. 464–483). Sage.

Vobič, I., & Trivundža, I. (2015). The Tyranny of the Empty Frame: Reluctance to Use Citizen-Produced Photographs in Online Journalism. *Journalism Practice*, 9(4): 502–519.

Vos, T.P. (2020). Journalists as Gatekeepers. In Wahl-Jorgensen, K. & Hanitzsch, T. (Eds.), *The Sage Handbook of Journalism Studies* (pp. 90–104). Routledge.

Waisbord, S. (2018). Truth Is What Happens to News. *Journalism Studies*, 19(13): 1866–1878.

Williams, K. (2006). Competing Models of Journalism? Anglo-american and European Reporting in the Information Age. *Journalistica*, 2: 43–65.

Zarzycka, M., & Kleppe, M. (2013). Awards, Archives, and Affects: Tropes in the World Press Photo contest 2009–11. *Media, Culture & Society*, 35(8): 977–995.

Zelizer, B. (2010). *About to Die: How News Images Move the Public*. Oxford University Press.

Zelizer, B. (2005). Death in Wartime: Photographs and the “Other War” in Afghanistan. *The Harvard International Journal of Press/Politics*, 10(3): 26–55.

Zelizer, B. (2007). On ‘having been there’: ‘Eyewitnessing’ as a Journalistic Keyword. *Critical Studies in Media Communication*, 24(5): 408–428.

Zelizer, B. (2008). Why Memory’s Work on Journalism Does Not Reflect Journalism’s Work on Memory. *Memory Studies*, 1(1): 79–87.

Index

For Product Safety Concerns and Information please contact our EU representative GPSR@taylorandfrancis.com
Taylor & Francis Verlag GmbH, Kaufingerstraße 24, 80331 München, Germany

www.ingramcontent.com/pod-product-compliance
Lightning Source LLC
LaVergne TN
LVHW020645100826
845148LV00012B/2346

* 9 7 8 1 0 3 2 7 6 3 3 4 7 *